ISLAND GARDENS

ISLAND GARDENS

Jackie Bennett

Photographs by Richard Hanson

WHITE
LION
PUBLISHING

Contents

Introduction 6

ISLES OF SCILLY 12

Tresco Abbey Garden 18
TRESCO
Echiums 22

THE SOUTH-WESTERN ISLES OF SCOTLAND 32

Brodick Castle 36
ARRAN

Ascog Hall 42
BUTE
King Fern 47

Achamore Gardens 50
GIGHA
The Horlick Rhododendrons 53

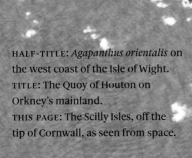

HALF-TITLE: *Agapanthus orientalis* on the west coast of the Isle of Wight.
TITLE: The Quoy of Houton on Orkney's mainland.
THIS PAGE: The Scilly Isles, off the tip of Cornwall, as seen from space.

CHANNEL ISLANDS 96

La Bigoterie 102
GUERNSEY

Herm Island 108
HERM
Wild Leek 111

La Seigneurie Gardens 112
SARK
Rosa Mundi 118

INNER HEBRIDES 122

Lip Na Cloiche 126
MULL

Priory Garden 138
ORONSAY
Wild Flowers 143

An Cala 144
SEIL

ANGLESEY: YNYS MÔN 56

Plas Cadnant 60
Himalayan Lily 71

ORKNEY 74

The Quoy of Houton 78
MAINLAND

Fiddlers Green 84
SOUTH RONALDSAY

Kierfiold House 86
MAINLAND
Hardy Geraniums on Orkney 91

ISLE OF WIGHT 152

Mottistone Gardens 156
Agapanthus 163

Crab Cottage 164

HOLY ISLAND 172

Lindisfarne Castle 176
Gertrude Jekyll's Flowering Annuals 185

Travel and Garden Guide 186
Index 189
Acknowledgments 192

Introduction

Ever since I could remember . . . flowers have been like dear friends to me, comforters, inspirers, powers to uplift and to cheer. A lonely child, living on the lighthouse island ten miles away from the mainland, every blade of grass that sprang out of the ground, every humblest weed, was precious in my sight.

Celia Thaxter, *An Island Garden*, 1894

IT WAS A LIGHTHOUSE KEEPER'S daughter, living in the Isles of Shoals, off the east coast of America, who gave us perhaps the most poignant account of what it is like to live on an island and to create a garden. Poet and gardener Celia Thaxter - as a child growing up on White Island and later as hostess of her father's hotel on Appledore, epitomized the pioneering spirit that is still embodied by those who make island gardens.

At its simplest, an island is a body of land surrounded by water, yet the word has become imbued with so many other meanings. In our minds, an island fulfils a universal need for escape, solace, beauty and isolation - all qualities that can also be found in a garden.

Until the mid-twentieth century, there were thousands of occupied lighthouses where the keeper and family lived. Perched on the edge of the sea, on a rock or other small islet, the lighthouse keeper would be at his station for months, sometimes years, at a time. Producing food for immediate needs would be the main concern and, perhaps, growing a few flowers for pleasure. In the British Isles, when the last manned lighthouse was automated in the 1990s, the final remnants of those particular island gardens disappeared too. Fortunately, lighthouse gardens are just a tiny proportion of gardens made on islands.

Island gardens are not necessarily seaside gardens - they have a wide range of aspects, from shady dells to sunny

On Scotland's west coast, Lismore lighthouse on Eilean Musdile, guides travellers into the Sound of Mull.

banks, deep-soiled, productive plots to rocky, alpine slopes. What they all share is the special light and atmosphere that proximity to water can bring. Crucially, they also have each had, at some time in their history, an owner or gardener who was determined to do what others consider impossible.

Off the north-west coast of Canada, in the early 1900s, Jennie Butchart turned her husband's redundant limestone quarry on Vancouver Island into an amazing sunken garden, now known as The Butchart Gardens. There is the floral extravaganza of Mainau Island on Lake Constance in the south-west of Germany, with its Baroque castle and arboretum created mainly by the grand dukes of Baden. Even in the North Sea, on the North Frisian islands, the caretakers of the little houses on Sylt have made pretty cottage gardens.

Britain has more visitable island gardens than anywhere else in the world, both on the larger inhabited islands of the Isle of Wight and Anglesey and on the smaller ones, particularly those off the Scottish coast, which are less populated and arguably more horticulturally challenging. The British Isles, in fact, consists of more than 6,000 individual islands. More than a hundred of these offshore islands are inhabited – and where there are people there are gardens. Gardeners are, by nature, optimists, and no extent of gales, storms and wet weather can deter them.

Island life may have drawbacks for gardeners, but it also has some unexpected bonuses – the long hours of sunshine on the Isle of Wight for example (more than 2,000 hours in an average year) or the temperature uplift provided by the Gulf Stream to gardens on the west coast of Scotland. Such meteorological quirks give island gardeners a chance to grow a range of plants that mainlanders cannot.

OPPOSITE: Many islands such as St Michael's Mount, with its castle and gardens, were originally religious settlements.
ABOVE: Sark is one of eight inhabited Channel Islands lying between the coast of northern France and southern England.

CLOSE CONNECTIONS

Thus, islands often have more in common with each other than with their nearest mainland. The reliance on cargo and supplies bought by ship is one obvious factor, and there is a thread running through this book of owners receiving plants from around the world - either by seeking them out themselves on plant-hunting expeditions or by commissioning ship captains to bring them back. Sometimes, as in the case of large tree ferns and palms, these would be used as ship ballast when the vessel returned to port empty of its original cargo. Heavy materials, rocks and gravel arrived in the same way - although today this is prohibitively expensive for most island gardeners.

The other factor that binds these gardens together is the wind. Each garden may have different temperatures, different amounts of rainfall and varying levels of sunshine, but the wind is almost always the element cited by island gardeners as their number one problem. How do you grow tall, tender or climbing plants when gale-force winds and salt damage are a certainty? The answer is hedging, and to talk to an island gardener is to continuously discuss the height of hedges, the types of hedges and even how many rows of hedges will be needed to protect the garden plants.

People determinedly growing the plants they really love is the essential subject of this book. Not surprisingly, the same plants turn up in very different geographical locations. *Geranium maderense* is one such plant; it could be taken as a totem for island gardeners. It comes from Madeira - a Portuguese island off Africa - where it thrives beneath the primary forests of the Laurisilva. On the Channel Islands, *G. maderense* is so ubiquitous that it is known as the Guernsey pink, and a white version, *G.m.* 'Guernsey White', is now commercially available. It is also a stalwart of Scilly, where it self-seeds freely, even clinging to sides of palm trees. On several Scottish islands, *G. maderense* was shown to me growing in a container, outdoors, as a 'badge of courage'.

Echiums have a similar cross-island appeal (see Echiums, page 22). *Echium candicans,* the shrubby echium known as the pride of Madeira, grows outdoors in Scilly as well as on the

Scottish Hebrides. Norfolk Island pines (*Araucaria heterophylla*) from the Pacific and Canary island date palms (*Phoenix canariensis*) from Gran Canaria are both familiar features of British island gardens. Then there was the Reverend David Landsborough, theologian, botanist and expert on seaweeds, who brought back the Chusan palm (*Trachycarpus fortunei*) from China to the village of Corrie, a seaside community on the Isle of Arran in Scotland, where he spent his holidays and where the plant's descendants still thrive.

A SIMPLER LIFE

Now turn the clock back 1,600 years to the time when the Christian religion was arriving on British shores, and islands figured large in the history of settlement and conversion. This led to religious centres on Iona, Oronsay, Lindisfarne and Caldey Island, where different monastic orders were established from the sixth century onwards. Historically, the monks and nuns grew food as a necessity and some of these gardens have since been reinvented for the modern world.

Even without the presence of a religious community, islands somehow hint at a simpler life. They promise something different, something slower, something outside of our everyday experience. Through long winters, an island garden can be a beacon of hope. 'Soon,' wrote Celia Thaxter:

> will set in the fitful weather, with fierce gales and sullen skies and frosty air, and it will be time to tuck up safely my Roses and Lilies . . . for their long winter sleep beneath the snow, where I never forget them, but ever dream of their wakening in happy summers yet to be.

For this reason, it is important to cherish what island gardens represent, and to applaud the gardeners who create beauty in the most unlikely places.

OPPOSITE: The Clachan bridge - known by locals as the Atlantic bridge - links the Isle of Seil with mainland Scotland. It is one of the shortest island crossings.
TOP RIGHT: The machair above the shore on South Ronaldsay is a treasure trove of wild flowers in spring.
CENTRE RIGHT: *Geranium maderense* grows freely across many of the islands of Britain.
BOTTOM RIGHT: Gorse and sea pinks (*Armeria maritima*) grow on the cliff tops of Gigha.

ISLES OF SCILLY

ALTHOUGH LYING JUST 45 kilometres/28 miles from Land's End, Scilly feels like a world away from the rest of the UK - balmy, Mediterranean even, certainly not 'British' in terms of weather or vegetation. Ask any gardener on Scilly what are their problem 'weeds' and they will immediately name agapanthus and echiums. Gardeners in other zones might be happy to coax such plants into flower but would probably have difficulty growing them.

The 200 isles of Scilly - five of which are inhabited (St Mary's, St Martin's, St Agnes, Bryher and Tresco) - are a product of rising sea levels that gradually cut them off, first from France and Spain, and then from Cornwall. Their final separation into individual islands may not have come until the sixteenth century, when rising tides, followed by some spectacular inundations of water in the early seventeenth century, left the islands more or less as we know them today, surrounded by shallow, turquoise seas. This process is still ongoing and Scilly has many 'tied' islands - those connected to each other by sand spits which are subject to change.

ISLAND FLORA

Were it not for Scilly's gardeners and the plants they have introduced, the character of the flora would be very different to the one we see today. The islands are part of a hard granite outcrop that stretches from Dartmoor out into the Atlantic Ocean. On top of that granite, the soil is mostly thin and acidic, a natural home to heathland plants, gorse, birch, a few elms and some nationally rare flora such as the dwarf pansy (*Viola kitaibeliana*) and Babington's leek (*Allium ampeloprasum* var. *babingtonii*). However, what really defines the islands are the alien plants that have made their home there: Bermuda buttercup (*Oxalis pes-caprae*) from South Africa; *Gladiolus communis* subsp. *byzantinus* from the Mediterranean; giant tree echium (*Echium*

PREVIOUS PAGES: St Martin's, with its white beaches and shallow waters, is one of the five inhabited isles of Scilly.
LEFT: Agapanthus now grows wild on the dunes and grasslands of Scilly; it was introduced in the 1850s by the proprietor of Tresco.

pininana) and its hybrids from the Canary Islands (see Echiums, page 22); and tree lupin (*Lupinus arboreus*) from California. Scilly is a gathering place for much more than just the early daffodils (*Narcissus*) for which it has become best known.

DAFFODILS

The multi-headed Tazetta daffodil known as *Narcissus* 'Scilly White' has been grown in Scilly for as long as anyone can remember, but it was in the latter half of the nineteenth century that flowers became a cash crop for the islands. Individual bulb farmers raised early daffodils in small, rectangular fields hedged with *Pittosporum crassifolium*, to protect them from the wind. They did well in the mild winters with good rainfall, and flowers could be picked from late autumn onwards. The scented blooms were packed in wooden crates and sent to Covent Garden, attracting high prices in London florists.

By the 1950s, there were around a hundred flower farms across Scilly; now there are less than ten. St Mary's, along with St Agnes, is home to most of the bulb growers today who have massed together to help combat competition from imported flowers. Cooperation is a byword in this island culture. No single farmer can produce enough flowers at the right time to satisfy the market, but together farmers can fill gaps and make the industry viable.

Traditionally, the most prolific bulb is the old French Tazetta *Narcissus* 'Soleil d'Or', which is the earliest to flower. However, by growing other cultivars such as *N.* 'Grand Primo', *N.* 'Moon Shadow', *N.* 'Matador' crosses, *N.* 'Golden Dawn' and *N.* 'Geranium', farmers are able to continue picking from late autumn to mid-spring.

As the trend for home-grown flowers increases, family-run farms such as Churchtown on the tiny island of St Martin's are giving year-round employment to fifteen or more people by growing two crops - daffodils in winter and scented pinks (*Dianthus*) in summer. Although methods have changed in some aspects, the small field sizes have not. On

this 14 hectare/34 acre farm, about 2 hectares/5 acres of land is ever in bulb production. The bulbs are grown on a four-year traditional rotation. The first year after planting, the crop is left to bulk up, followed by three years of hand picking. Then the bulbs are lifted, divided and the best bulbs replanted in a different field. The first field is sown with stubble turnip, followed by grass and clover ley for grazing the farm's herd of beef cattle. Hay is cut twice a year for the cattle to complete the cycle, without the need for any chemical fertilizers.

Picking is always done by hand, when the flowers are still in tight bud, usually three days a week to keep a continuous supply. If you see a field of daffodils fully open on Scilly, it is probably an old field, or one in its first year's 'rest'.

Traditionally, the crop is grown on ridges to allow a good depth of soil. New bulbs are sterilized with hot water before planting. Although this cuts down on pests and diseases, it can cause the first-year flowers to be damaged, but it doesn't affect them in later years. Because these bulbs originate from a Mediterranean environment where fires are common, the fields are deliberately set alight on a dry day. The combination of heat and smoke removes all traces of the old leaves and helps to control weeds.

The hedges are as important a part of bulb cultivation as the burning, lifting and dividing. Great care is given to their upkeep, because without them the crops would be prey to gale-force winds, laden with salt. Pittosporum is the most common hedging choice, but olearia is also used - both evergreens which typically enclose three sides of the sloping fields. Euonymus is another important hedging plant on Scilly, being sturdy and frost resistant, if slower growing than pittosporum and olearia. Escallonia has been tried on the islands but is not popular in a place where every small piece of land is precious, mainly because it is too hungry and thirsty, making the ground in its lee dry and uncultivatable.

OPPOSITE: The small Scilly fields are hedged with evergreen pittosporum to shelter the flowers from the sea winds and salt spray.
RIGHT: Narcissus 'Golden Dawn' is a multi-headed, scented Tazetta, good for picking.

Tresco Abbey Garden

For many travellers, the ultimate destination on Scilly is the island of Tresco. At 3.2 kilometres/2 miles long, it punches way above its size in terms of horticultural influence. The promise of seeing a flowering paradise all year round in the British Isles is irresistible, and plant lovers come to Tresco Abbey Garden from far and wide.

Everything about Tresco is familiar and yet rather strange. Golden pheasants walk the garden paths and red-legged partridge forage on the beach. Red squirrels, fearing no predators, sit and have their photos taken without so much as a twitch. Only rabbits are discouraged - although everyone agrees it's a thankless task to try to eradicate them.

At Tresco Abbey Garden the seasons mean little. On New Year's Day, there can be 300 plants in flower including *Choisya ternata*, acacias, hebes, pelargoniums and salvias - none of them under glass - and this ebb and flow of flowering and leaf pays little heed to what is going on in the rest of the British Isles. In mid-spring, *Geranium maderense* from Madeira is in full bloom, alongside clivias, proteas, aeoniums and the first stems of agapanthus. Throughout summer, there will be daturas, aloes, more proteas, banksias and so on. By late autumn, only the bare branches of the deciduous elms give a clue that this is mid-winter, in Britain.

Usually tagged as 'subtropical', Tresco Abbey actually has a cool temperate climate - even Scilly doesn't get anything approaching tropical heat in the summer months. That tropical feel is, however, enhanced by the surrounding shallow seas, white sands and palm trees.

The garden's good fortune is that it does not suffer the typical ups and downs of the British weather; frosts are rare and temperatures vary by around 9°C/16°F between winter and summer. Sunshine levels are high, but the wind stops temperatures from soaring. As a result, the garden takes its

From the top of Tresco Abbey Garden the main island of St Mary's is clearly visible.

inspiration from the five zones that share this Mediterranean climate: the Mediterranean basin itself; Central Chile; the Western Cape of South Africa; California and south-western and southern Australia.

It is a garden where generations of gardeners have collected seeds and plants from around the world, facilitated by the proximity of the sea and close relationship with ocean-going vessels and their crews.

SALTY TALES

The story of Tresco Abbey Garden begins in 1834 when Augustus Smith took over the ninety-nine-year lease of the Isles of Scilly from the Duchy of Cornwall. He was a controversial lord proprietor - committed to eradicating smuggling and introducing compulsory education for Scilly's children - neither of which was popular at the time. He decided to make

his home on Tresco, partly because it offered the most privacy, but also because of its situation, being encircled by several other islands that protect it from the elements.

Augustus built himself a large house and then set about the garden on a 7-hectare/17-acre site, firstly around and within the ruins of the tenth-century Benedictine abbey. A shelter belt of Monterey cypress (*Cupressus macrocarpa*) and Monterey pines (*Pinus radiata*) was planted in the 1850s, which grew quickly and also helped to shut out the Atlantic winds and salt-laden spray.

Many generations of the family played a part, including Thomas Algernon Dorrien-Smith, who oversaw the rise of the bulb industry, and Major A.A. Dorrien-Smith, a renowned horticulturist. They continued the tradition of Tresco owners of travelling abroad in search of plants to bring home. It is hard sometimes not to think of Tresco Abbey as a botanic or public

garden, but it was – and is – a very exciting private garden, created by passionate and knowledgeable owners and staff.

Since 1985 the garden has been in the care of Mike Nelhams, the garden curator who works with his team under Robert A. Dorrien-Smith. This continuity of care is something central to the ethos of Tresco. For three decades, Mike along with his head gardener Andrew Lawson and a small but key team of professionals – a propagator, kitchen gardener and three students annually – maintain and develop this special place.

NATURAL CHALLENGES

The layout of the gardens remains very much as Augustus Smith had planned it, with the terraces working down the slope, paths cutting across from east to west and the dominating Neptune steps, which descend from north to south and are named after the ship's figurehead that sits at the top.

Amazing as Tresco is in terms of the sheer abundance and variety of unusual plants, there are some very strict parameters within which this garden has to operate. The rainfall, for example, is plentiful in winter but can be modest in summer, and there is no automatic watering system. The soil is by nature moorland and acidic peat, a free-draining sandy loam, which has been greatly improved over the past two centuries. Even within the 'Tresco' microclimate there are a series of specific microclimates. The top terrace, which is dry and has no access to water, is used to grow plants from Australia and Mexico including proteas, aloes, agaves and clivias, which enjoy such

OPPOSITE: Tresco Abbey has been the home of the Dorrien-Smith family since 1834.
BELOW: The original garden was made around the ruins of a Benedictine priory.

ECHIUMS

Echiums are naturalized on many British islands, where they have escaped from gardens – and, of course, lots of gardeners like to grow them. *Echium pininana* is the most familiar; this giant of a plant in the right conditions, and a relative of the native viper's bugloss (*E. vulgare*), is commonly known as the giant tree echium. In its Canary Island home, the giant tree echium would be a biennial producing a rosette of foliage in its first year, followed by the flower spike in the second year. On Tresco it is biennial, but farther north on the western islands of Scotland it sometimes takes longer to flower – becoming a triennial, even a quadrennial. Gardeners there believe that if something is worth growing it's worth waiting for.

There is an ongoing battle to win a record for the tallest echiums grown outdoors in the British Isles. Tresco and Herm would all have good candidates – 4m/13ft is common where winters are mild. Where winters are cold, however, these plants need to spend their first winter under the cover of a cool greenhouse.

Plants grown on the milder west coasts of Britain and Ireland self-seed very successfully, leading to echiums being considered almost a weed in some places. Being a member of the borage family, they have very spiny stems and bristly leaves, but are robust and very good for attracting bees and butterflies.

The bush echium (*E. candicans*), known as the pride of Madeira, is a more compact species, a multi-stemmed subshrub that is also biennial in most gardens, but growing to a more manageable 2m/7ft tall. Across Tresco and within the Abbey Garden, these shrub echiums have crossed naturally with tree echiums to produce *E.* x *scilloniensis*, which are tall, open, multi-headed plants.

LEFT: Giant tree echium (*E. pininana*)
ABOVE: Bush echium (*E. candicans*)

conditions. Whereas at the bottom of the slope nearest the sea, where there is some shade and deeper soil, it is cooler and more moist and tree ferns thrive, providing shelter for plants on the middle terrace.

In 1987, the unthinkable happened. Scilly suffered temperatures of -8°C/17°F and 30cm/1ft of snow covered the garden. The snow lasted less than a week, but when paired with the wind-chill factor the temperatures plummeted for ten days or more, and little survived. Around 85 per cent of the plants did not recover.

Three years later in 1990, disaster struck again with a hurricane lasting just two hours, but bringing 205km/h/127mph winds that wiped out whatever had not been damaged by the 1987 snow. Not everything died at once - palms were knocked back severely while other plants such as banksias died slowly over several years.

As the team tried to work out what had survived, nature was working beneath their feet. Seeds of the palm heaths (*Richea pandanifolia*) had remained viable under the layer of snow, and were collected and grown on by other gardens around Britain that had offered to help Tresco. The gardeners found that as more light came into the garden there was an explosion of seed germination. They also spent six months plant

ABOVE: A cliff cut into the bedrock is home to succulents from around the world, including aeoniums, aloes and mesembryanthemums.
FOLLOWING PAGES: Looking down over the middle terrace, signature Canary Island date palms (*Phoenix canariensis*) tower over the paths.

collecting from botanical gardens around Britain. Tree ferns from Logan Botanic Garden in Scotland brought back some structure, while South African aloes from the Royal Botanic Garden Edinburgh and Chilean puya (*Puya chilensis*) from Maurice Mason's collection in Suffolk restored some of the exotic feel that had been lost. In seeking to repopulate what was in essence a bare hillside, Mike and his team travelled widely to make contacts with the Western Australian Botanic Garden, Kings Park in Perth, Huntington Botanic Garden in California and Kirstenbosch National Botanic Garden in South Africa.

The following years meant planting for shelter and continuous propagation by the team. It took twenty years to refill the garden but created lasting connections between Tresco and gardens in Britain and the rest of the world. As well as plant swapping, the gardeners formed great bonds of friendship and knowledge sharing, which is something that defines Tresco Abbey Garden today.

PLANTS AND PLANTING

The team kept a log of what died, what survived and what was planted, creating a comprehensive record of the garden's revival. In terms of trees, only the monkey puzzle (*Araucaria araucana*) trees had survived along with the holm oak (*Quercus ilex*) hedges. Most were cut back severely, including the cabbage trees (*Cordyline australis*) and Canary Island date palms (*Phoenix canariensis*). The garden we see today with its Norfolk Island pines (*Araucaria heterophylla*) and bright New Zealand Christmas trees (*Metrosideros excelsa*) is essentially one that has been created in the past three decades.

When a garden is subject to such an extensive replanting scheme – 60,000 new trees were put in after the 1987 storm and each one was no more than 45cm/18in tall to ensure it would not suffer wind rock – areas of repetition are inevitable. Now in the twenty-first century, attention has turned again to making the most of the garden's microclimates.

Although Tresco is a garden known for its plants, it is not a garden of plant 'collections' and this is something that

ABOVE LEFT: The central axis leads up to the Mediterranean Garden and gazebo.
LEFT: Water from the sculpture is pumped back down to the Mediterranean pool.
OPPOSITE: The interior of the gazebo was decorated with shells and mosaics by Lucy Dorrien-Smith.

ABOVE LEFT: *Osteospermum* 'Nairobi Purple' was collected by 'Commander Tom' – one of the plant-hunting Dorrien-Smiths in the mid-twentieth century.

ABOVE RIGHT: The Neptune steps were named after a ship's figurehead, which stands at the top of the steps.

RIGHT: Neptune originally belonged to a ship that was wrecked on the western rocks of Scilly in 1841.

successive head gardeners and owners have consciously resisted. Sometimes it is difficult to know where to draw the line - there are, for example, some 650 Cape heathers that *could* be grown and just about every protea in cultivation would do well there, but the goal is not to collect every known species or cultivar but just to continue to expand the genera within the garden.

There are some plants that specifically represent Tresco: *Olearia* × *scilloniensis*, for example, is a naturally occurring cross of olearia, which has taken off and is sold worldwide. *Osteospermum* 'Tresco Peggy' was brought back by 'Commander Tom', one of the plant-hunting Dorrien-Smiths - its official name is now *O.* 'Nairobi Purple'. However, the main aim is not to breed or cultivate Tresco plants. The guiding principle, initiated by the owners and previous gardeners such as Peter Clough (who also worked at Achamore Gardens; see page 50) is to continue to experiment with the plants that grow well there and study how they grow. Mike Nelhams and his team continually push the boundaries of what can succeed - bearing in mind that the

ABOVE LEFT: The figure of Gaia is one of several sculptures in the garden created by David Wynne.

ABOVE RIGHT: The upper terrace is home to *Geranium maderense*, echiums and other Mediterranean-zone plants that enjoy the warm conditions.

plants won't be continually watered or nurtured under glass. Everything at Tresco is propagated to go outdoors - there are no show houses of tender plants.

The gardeners welcome self-seeders, which include aeoniums and the giant tree echiums - the tall, stately plant that grows everywhere on Scilly. These along with helichrysums, agapanthus, *Euphorbia mellifera* and crocosmias verge on the semi-wild and need to be controlled if they are not to crowd out the other plants. Even specialities such as the dandelion tree (*Sonchus arboreus*) need careful weeding to stop them sprouting everywhere. The gardeners are encouraged to take a real interest in this natural evolution and there is an ongoing project with the Eden Project in Cornwall, which grows specific plants under glass while Tresco grows the same ones outdoors.

Tresco has always been about people as much as plants. Because Mike Nelhams went to Tresco Abbey Garden first as a student, horticultural students are very much encouraged to spend time there, learning what this particular mix of climate and landscape has to offer. Every year, the garden staff visit gardens on the Riviera to renew their acquaintance with the Mediterranean zone. For 180 years, Tresco Abbey has been at the epicentre of horticulture initiative - not bad for a once barren, sheep-grazed island, way out in the Celtic Sea.

BELOW: The blue bridge is a recent addition to the garden, welcoming twenty-first century visitors to the Abbey Garden.
OPPOSITE CLOCKWISE FROM TOP LEFT: *Puya chilensis*, *Protea neriifolia*, *Aeonium canariense*, *Leucospermum cordifolium*, *Aeonium arboreum* 'Atropurpureum', *Argyranthemum* hybrid, *Aloe polyphylla*, *Beschorneria yuccoides*, *Cordyline australis* Purpurea Group.

THE SOUTH-WESTERN
ISLES OF SCOTLAND

ARRAN AND BUTE are islands of the Firth of Clyde, belonging to an area of lochs, sea and peninsulas in the south-west of Scotland now known as Argyle and Bute. For generations of Glaswegians Bute and Arran have been their island getaways - Bute accessed by a boat trip down the river Clyde and just far enough from the mainland to make it seem a little bit remote and magical. Arran, too, is reached by boat in less than an hour, although it perhaps seems a bit more adventurous. The third island included in this chapter - Gigha - is less visited and more remote. It lies on the outer flank of the Kintyre peninsula, and involves just a short sea crossing but many hours of road travel to get to the crossing point at Tayinloan.

These islands have a more protected climate than some of the Outer Hebridean islands of Scotland, and as such have been sought out by wealthy gardeners of the nineteenth century looking for somewhere to settle and grow plants. They also share a common gardening heritage - of nineteenth-century owners who were far more obsessed with their gardens than with their houses.

CLIMATE AND VEGETATION

On Arran, huge climatic changes over time have settled down to give the island moderately mild winters, influenced by the North Atlantic Drift - the northern extension of the Gulf Stream - and high rainfall caused by the prevailing south-westerly winds. The lowland peninsula of Kintyre does nothing to stop those winds which, when they meet the peaks of Arran, deposit 2m/7ft of rainfall per year.

Apart from the high granite peaks, a blanket of peat exists over most of the island, along with pockets of boulder clay. Were it not for the intervention of man on Arran, the tree cover would be relatively sparse. Arran has its own native service tree, *Sorbus arranensis*, which is remarkable for surviving on almost no soil, putting its roots directly into the granite. Birch and oaks will grow to 460m/1,500ft, leaving gorse, heather, bilberry, saxifrages, sedges and purple moor grass (*Molinia caerulea*; *Ciob* in Gaelic) to colonize the higher slopes. Lower down, the planted trees include beech, chestnut, limes and Scots pine as well as plantations of conifers in places. Near sea level, in the villages, the plots are cultivated and hedged with hawthorn, holly or *Fuchsia* 'Riccartonii'.

Bute's main town of Rothesay was once a great late nineteenth- and early twentieth-century holiday destination. Thousands of visitors came to see what the seaside did best: splendid buildings (such as the Winter Gardens and an elaborate and highly decorated Victorian public conveniences - both now restored), as well as brilliantly colourful bedding-plant displays set out behind the wide esplanade.

Although it is not what it was, that legacy of Bute as a 'garden isle' remains, but with rather less of the razzmatazz. Crowds are more likely to arrive by cruise ship than Clyde paddle steamer, and they usually head straight for Mount Stuart, the 3rd Marquess of Bute's astonishing homage to the Gothic Revival movement. The grounds include an eighteenth-century parkland, a late nineteenth-century rockery designed by Thomas Mawson and a mainly twentieth-century kitchen garden with contributions from designers Rosemary Verey and James Alexander-Sinclair.

The other draw for day trippers to Bute is the much-loved annual planting schemes laid out by the gardeners of the Argyll and Bute Council. The headquarters is at Ardencraig Gardens, where petunias and pelargoniums are grown in profusion in the glasshouses. The walled gardens were originally part of Ardencraig House but were acquired by Rothesay Town Council and latterly by Argyll and Bute Council. This knowledge of glasshouse growing is still very much valued in the town, and both locals and visitors make the steep climb up the hill behind the town to watch the succession of colour from late spring onwards. It may be a fading coastal tradition, but the expertise that goes with raising annuals and bedding plants is being nurtured at Ardencraig.

Gigha cannot compete with Arran or Bute in terms of size or visitor numbers, but its terrain is perfect for garden making - being low lying and fertile. It is the site of one of the most atmospheric island gardens, known as Achamore Garden (see page 50).

PREVIOUS PAGES: Arran is often known as 'Scotland in miniature' because of its combination of highland and lowland landscapes.
OPPOSITE: Brodick Castle sits below Goat Fell, the highest point on Arran, at 874m/2,867ft.

Brodick Castle

ARRAN

On a raised plateau above Arran's eastern shore sits Brodick Castle, beneath the island's highest peak, Goat Fell (*Gaoda Bheinn* in Gaelic) at 874m/2,867ft. It has a defensive history stretching back to the thirteenth century enhanced by its position as a lookout point across the Firth of Clyde.

Brodick's horticultural story, however, begins in the nineteenth century, with the marriage of the 11th Duke of Hamilton to Princess Marie of Baden in 1843. This couple moved into the renovated castle in the 1840s and during Princess Marie's time the upper parts of the garden were terraced and the house extended in the Scottish Baronial style by James Gillespie Graham. In an attempt to recreate the wooded environment of her *Schwarzwald* home, Princess Marie's husband constructed four elaborate summerhouses made of rhododendron stems and decorated with pine cones; sadly, only one survives.

The sloping upper walled garden, originally built as a kitchen garden in 1710, was found to be too 'visible' from the house and was converted in the 1840s into a pleasure garden. A very old bay laurel (*Laurus nobilis*) might well be a remnant of the old productive garden, which was moved to a flatter area away from view.

It was the 12th Duke's only child, Lady Marie Louise Hamilton, who inherited the house in 1895 (and became, by marriage in 1906, the Duchess of Montrose) and who made most impact on the gardens we see today. She was fascinated with, and subscribed to, the plant-hunting expeditions of the 1920s undertaken by George Forrest, Joseph Rock and Frank Kingdon-Ward. (In the 1960s, a collection of Kingdon-Ward plants was discovered by head gardener John Basford, including specimens of almost every introduction from Kingdon-Ward's 1953 'Triangle' expedition to Upper Burma.) Together with her son-in-law Major J.P.T. Boscawen and a team of gardeners, the duchess began to create a woodland garden, initially with a gift

The sloping walled garden was originally built as a kitchen garden but was changed to a pleasure garden in the 1840s.

ABOVE: The gardens at Brodick owe much to the Duchess of Montrose, who inherited Brodick in 1895.

RIGHT: The upper part of the walled garden still contains some of the original plants brought from Tresco on behalf of the duchess.

OPPOSITE: The lower slopes are favourable for the majority of the rhododendron collection, as well as the trees from South America.

of *Rhododendron magnificum* and other plants from Muncaster Castle in Cumbria.

Major Boscawen organized a whole steamship of plants to be brought in from Tresco Abbey Garden (see page 18). Cabbage palm (*Cordyline australis*) as well as fine mature specimens of *C. banksii* and *C. indivisa* are planted on the upper terraces. Lower down the garden, where the soil is deeper and more acid, the woodland was enhanced with camellias and rhododendrons, along with Chilean fire bush (*Embothrium coccineum*), rare southern beeches (*Nothofagus*) and the lily-of-the-valley tree (*Clethra arborea*).

But the west coast of Scotland is not Tresco: the winters are not always totally frost-free at Brodick, although prolonged sub-zero temperatures are rare. Agaves and bananas (*Musa*) need wrapping with fleece, although generally it is just the crowns that need protection rather than the whole plant. The combination of rain and relative mildness has allowed plants from Chile, Burma, the Himalayas and Tasmania to flourish and give this garden its lush, jungle-like feel.

Thanks to the Duchess of Montrose, who passed the castle and its 32 hectares/80 acres of gardens to the National Trust for Scotland in 1957, and her daughter Lady Jean Fforde, who grew up at Brodick Castle, it is rhododendrons for which the gardens are renowned. There are 400 different species and more than 200 hybrids, covering almost all of the world's subsections – getting on for 2,000 individual rhododendron plants. The huge-leaved *Rhododendron macabeanum* and *R. montroseanum* (named after the duchess) thrive on the lower slopes whereas the upper west side is more favourable for the scented collection (*R.* Subsection *Maddenii*), one of three National Collections held here – the other two being the large-leaved *R.* Subsection *Falconeri* and *R.* Subsection *Grandia*.

The gardeners and volunteers at Brodick Castle are often tasked with removing its most troublesome weed, *Griselinia littoralis*, which is a shiny-leaved, evergreen shrub introduced as a good barrier against salt and wind, but which seeds so prolifically that any bare piece of earth will soon be covered by a carpet of its tough, bright green stems. Ironically, there is a

ABOVE: The pond is surrounded with large-leaved *Gunnera manicata*, *Primula pulverulenta* and tree ferns.

OPPOSITE: Some of Brodick Castle's diverse collection of rhododendrons; CLOCKWISE FROM TOP: *Rhododendron niveum*, *R. maddenii* hybrid, *R.* 'Glory of Littleworth', woodland paths overhung with rhododendrons, new growth on *R. macabeanum*, *R. augustinii* Electra Group 'Electra', *R. hemsleyanum*, *R. vernicosum* hybrid.

champion griselinia tree at Brodick Castle, which cannot be sacrificed no matter how many offspring it produces.

In the early 2000s, the fungal diseases *Phytophthora ramorum* and *P. kernoviae* arrived here and affected much of the lower garden. The shelter belt of *Rhododendron ponticum* was a casualty but the garden also lost a lot of shelter on the shore, including camellias, magnolias, crinodendrons and inevitably some of the choice rhododendrons. Fortunately, the garden has been free of *Phytophthora* since 2014 and, although replanting of the shelter belt has been a priority, it has also opened up opportunities for new planting.

In 1962, as the National Trust for Scotland were grappling with the extent of the plant collections, another garden was recognizing the importance of passing on its horticultural history. Sir James Horlick, a noted plant collector and breeder was in his late seventies and gifted a collection of his rhododendrons to many gardens, including Brodick Castle, for posterity and to ensure their survival. A garden on another island continues the rhododendron story: it is Achamore Gardens on the Isle of Gigha (see page 50).

Ascog Hall
BUTE

Sitting about half way between Rothesay and Mount Stuart is Ascog Hall, a garden with a great history, which has recently become one of the Royal Horticultural Society's (RHS) smallest Partner Gardens. Ascog Hall stands just above the shoreline, overlooking the Firth of Clyde, and was bought by the Stewart family in the 1850s. It ended up in the hands of Alexander Bannatyne Stewart who, although his origins were 'trade', brought a flourish of beauty and embellishment to what was a fairly austere house and garden. It is said that he never walked out in the town of Rothesay without a flower in his buttonhole - and a statue of him now stands on the esplanade to honour his good nature and philanthropic works.

Bannatyne Stewart is perhaps best described as a collector rather than a horticulturalist. He admired and collected firstly art and then orchids and, in due course, ferns. He commissioned the artist and illustrator Edward La Trobe Bateman to landscape the grounds and to build the unusual sunken glasshouse to house his collection. Bateman was acclaimed for drawing plans for the Royal Botanic and other gardens in Melbourne, Australia. He made Bute his home in 1869 and worked on the interiors of Mount Stuart as well as designing the fernery for Ascog Hall in 1870.

The Crown of Gold Fernery - so called because of its gilded-metal roof decoration - was an ambitious project. It had to be excavated to a depth of 2.9m (9½ft) so that the glazed iron roof would be at ground level. It was designed to be an unheated temperate house with the cave-like interior walls keeping the plants at a constant temperature. Soon after it was finished, it was written up in the *Gardeners' Chronicle* of 25 October 1879, with a complete inventory of the ferns. The discovery of this article spearheaded a push for restoration which, with the help of Historic Scotland, was completed in 1997. From the inventory, the Royal Botanic Garden Edinburgh was able to

Tree ferns, cordylines and other plants from the southern hemisphere thrive within the gardens at Ascog Hall.

ABOVE: The monkey puzzle tree is from the original nineteenth-century planting.
OPPOSITE: *Primula pulverulenta* flourishes in a bed around the formal pool.

restock it more or less accurately. The star then - as now - was the king fern (*Todea barbara*) (see page 47). It is the only survivor of the Victorian planting, and it is possibly one of the oldest ferns in cultivation.

Apart from a towering monkey puzzle (*Araucaria araucana*), there are few reminders of the garden's heyday, and so it has been left to each owner to make what they could of the steeply sloping site. In the late twentieth century this fell to the Fyfe family, who understood its difficult terrain - rocky and poor in places but in others deep and fertile - and realized that in these spots it was capable of growing interesting shrubs. The plants that do well in the mild winters and cool summers of Bute come from similar climatic zones, particularly Chile, the Himalayas and New Zealand.

In 2014, Ascog came into the care of Karin and Michael Burke, who were looking for an active retirement project. They certainly got that, and in their first three years they rebuilt the back of the Grade-B-listed house, which had almost collapsed, and set about the garden. It is hard to overstate the personal input in this 1.2-hectare/3-acre plot. German-born Karin was not fazed by an overgrown historic garden and Michael enjoyed the physical labour after years behind a computer, and he threw himself into sorting out the drainage issues - channelling three natural watercourses into rills and small streams. The hill behind the garden offers some protection from the prevailing (west) wind, but it also funnels all the rainfall, sweeping fertile soil down to the bottom.

ABOVE: The sunken fernery was designed by Edward La Trobe Bateman in 1870.

RIGHT: The ground was excavated to 2.75m/9ft deep, in order to create the perfect conditions for temperate ferns.

KING FERN

Estimated to be already 1,000 years old in the late nineteenth century, the king fern (*Todea barbara*) stands today at the back of Ascog's fernery, the only remnant of the original planting. An article in the *Gardeners' Chronicle* of October 1879 described seeing it for the first time:

> The most wonderful plant is a Todea Africana, the stem or trunk of which is 5 feet high, 5 feet in diameter, and 15 feet round; it has one hundred fronds, which are about 12 feet across, and it is said to be a thousand years old or more. It is the most wonderful Fern I have ever seen . . .

However, when restoration of the fernery started in 1997 there was just one single frond left on the king fern, but now it is thriving again and thought to be the oldest specimen in cultivation. Indigenous to South Africa, Australia and New Zealand, king fern is increasingly rare in the wild. Its natural habitat is on the edge of forests and beside streams, yet it seems happy in the moist, unheated glasshouse at Ascog Hall. Its survival against the odds must in part be credited to the original owner's gardener, Mr Todd, who collected and arranged the rocks in the fernery and attentively tended the fern collection for Bannatyne Stewart. There seems to be no connection between Todd and *Todea* (the name given to the king fern officially in 1854), so perhaps the fern's name is just a happy coincidence.

ABOVE RIGHT: The fernery, as depicted in 1879.

RIGHT: King fern (*Todea barbara*)

Although they worried about the responsibility of caring for the historic fernery, there was a regime already in place - yearly visits from experts from the British Pteridological Society and monitoring by the Royal Botanic Garden Edinburgh as well as a volunteer neighbour, Neil Owen, who undertakes the crucial watering for one and a half hours, every day.

If gardeners make gardens then gardens can also make gardeners. As the Burkes uncovered more and more unusual plants from other temperate zones, their interest grew and they began to realize the garden was quite special. On the damp meadow lawn, three different native hardy orchids were discovered, including the vulnerable lesser butterfly orchid (*Platanthera bifolia*). Their interest has expanded particularly towards Chilean plants. They added to the existing trees and shrubs and now have a thriving Chilean community: for example, winter's bark (*Drimys winteri*), Chilean fire bush (*Embothrium coccineum*) and Chilean lantern tree (*Crinodendron hookerianum*). Karin became fascinated with the stories behind plants, and visitors can now follow the journeys of plant hunters such as David Douglas who, after introducing the Douglas fir (*Pseudotsuga menziesii*) to Scotland, died in a bull pit in Hawaii, or Archibald Menzies who, while on official business in Chile in 1795, was served nuts from the monkey puzzle tree for dessert, and hid them away in his pocket to bring back to Britain.

Like every garden, Ascog Hall has its share of problems. When the Burkes first arrived, deer wandered in from above and below until the plot was fenced and gated. And there are 'weeds' - here it is Himalayan honeysuckle (*Leycesteria formosa*), with its seed pods that explode and distribute everywhere. Even the lovely Californian tree poppy (*Romneya coulteri*) is so prolific in the mild climate that it has to be removed.

The Burkes needed to attract more people to the garden to fund its upkeep and in 2016 Ascog Hall became an RHS Partner Garden - at the time it was one of about twenty-five in Scotland. Making a historic garden work for twenty-first century family life is the balancing act for Ascog Hall. The Burkes inherited no records or historic documents and have no public funding. This is a garden where each generation has added and subtracted and each owner has had to be part-archaeologist, part-horticulturalist, and always to acknowledge that a garden is, by nature, a work in progress.

OPPOSITE FROM TOP:
Meconopsis (Fertile Blue Group) 'Lingholm', *Embothrium coccineum*, *Crinodendron hookerianum*.

ABOVE: Spring-flowering magnolias and a variegated maple (*Acer*) are underplanted with ferns and hostas.

LEFT: A narrow gravel path winds between *Acer palmatum* 'Atropurpureum' and the sweet-smelling yellow azalea (*Rhododendron luteum*).

Achamore Gardens
GIGHA

Just 5 kilometres/3 miles from the Scottish mainland, across the Sound of Gigha, a small 'Loch-class' ferry takes a few cars and passengers each day to a narrow island that lies parallel to the peninsula of Kintyre. On arrival, Gigha is nowhere near as striking as Arran, appearing as a gentle ridge of fertile land and measuring less than 1.6 kilometres/1 mile wide in places. On a fine day, you can clearly see the mountains of its neighbours: the Paps of Jura to the west, Goat Fell on Arran to the east and sometimes Beinn Mhòr on Mull, 80 kilometres/50 miles to the north.

Three factors make Gigha an ideal place to make a garden: its mild winters; the relatively low hills; and its lower rainfall – one-third to a half of the amount that falls on the higher lands of Kintyre and Arran. The Vikings named it 'The Good Isle'. It does, however, suffer from prevailing south-westerly winds and with no land masses to stop their force they can be strong. The soil is naturally very acid loam, but a long history of cultivation and grazing of small dairy herds has meant that where there should be only gorse, there are green pastures, small arable fields and woodlands.

Gigha has been on the horticultural map since Lt-Col. James Horlick (of the malted milk drinks company) bought the island in 1944, mainly to house his growing collection of temperate plants and, in particular, his rhododendrons. According to the locals, Horlick arrived on Gigha after a rocky boat ride from Islay, where he had been looking for a small estate to start his garden. He climbed off the tiny wooden ferry, lost his footing and claimed that he had 'slipped and fallen in love with Gigha'.

The house he chose to live in was Achamore, which had been remodelled in the first decades of the twentieth century by a team of architects that included Charles Rennie Mackintosh – then a young draughtsman working for the firm of Honeyman & Keppie in Glasgow and who had a hand in the Arts & Crafts

Planted by James Horlick in the 1940s, Achamore Gardens are a plant lover's paradise, particularly in spring.

interiors. Achamore House had everything a twentieth-century country gentleman could want: a 0.8 hectare/2 acre walled garden, carriage rides, terraced lawns and, most importantly, hectares of woodland, which could shelter his plants from the winds.

THE HORLICK YEARS

Horlick was not just a collector of interesting plants, he also bred around forty-eight rhododendron cultivars of his own, many of which have been identified as still growing at the gardens (see opposite). He recognized that within the gardens he could create a series of microclimates suitable for growing plants, which would be impossible at his other houses in Berkshire and Oxfordshire. He designed each garden specifically to hold individual groups of plants in little 'groves', using the existing trees and vegetation as protection. He was aided in this by Kitty

Lloyd Jones, whom Horlick described as a 'professional lady gardener', perhaps not giving her full credit for her involvement in Achamore Gardens. In fact, she helped him to locate the garden and then lived and worked there intermittently from 1944 to 1955. She probably had a personal relationship with Horlick and certainly helped in the design of the estimated one hundred individual garden spaces created there – some now lost within the encroaching woodland.

Each one of these garden spaces celebrated either a particular group of temperate plants or was named after people that Horlick knew. (Achamore's long-standing head gardener, Malcolm Allan, and Horlick's friend George Taylor both have areas of the garden named after them.) The names helped to distinguish areas within this 20-hectare/50-acre woodland: Fulvum Garden, for example (for the collection of *Rhododendron fulvum*); Falconeri Garden; and Macabeanum Wood. According to one of the gardeners who worked there in the late 1960s, Horlick would come into the garden and shout 'Has anyone seen Colonel Rogers?' referring to the pink rhododendron of that name. The only way to find your way about was to learn the names and locations of the plants.

Horlick ran a staff of eight to ten gardeners, with two allocated to the walled vegetable garden and glasshouses. The breeding work he had begun in Berkshire (including of the popular *R*. 'Mrs James Horlick', named after his first wife) continued and the rest of the gardeners were often put to propagation work. Malcolm MacNeill, who joined the garden staff as a fifteen-year-old boy in 1958 under head gardener Malcolm Allan, remembers air layering the rhododendrons and then – in the years before Gigha had a regular ferry crossing – he would travel with the precious packages on a lobster boat to Tarbert on the Kintyre peninsula. Here they were stored in a boat shed overnight before being transported by small fishing crafts to other gardens across Scotland – Glendoick, Crarae, Ardkinglas, Colonsay House, Inverewe, Lochranza and Brodick Castle (see page 36).

Horlick, who became a baronet in 1958, knew the importance of his collections and the network he had initiated. In 1962, he donated a collection of his plants to the National Trust for Scotland, as well as the sum of £25,000 to be used for

Achamore House was the home of twentieth-century plant collector and breeder James Horlick.

THE HORLICK RHODODENDRONS

James Horlick had begun crossing and raising rhododendrons from cuttings and layering at his home in Sunninghill in Berkshire. He was by no means a one-plant man, but he did have a special fondness for rhododendrons and two subsections in particular: *Maddenii*, which are scented and are considered a challenge for growers; and *Cinnabarina*, so called because the original plants were cinnabar-red.

He placed the less hardy *Maddenii* on the hillside at Achamore, where they would get less frost, whereas he grew *R. cinnabarinum* throughout the gardens, including those he called 'the ladies': *R.* 'Lady Berry', *R.* Lady Chamberlain Group and *R.* Lady Rosebery Group. Horlick raised at least fifty hybrids himself, including the dark red *R.* 'Leo' (*R.* 'Britannia' x *R. elliottii*) which he raised from a seed given to him in 1929 from Exbury gardens in Hampshire. His introductions include: *R.* 'Lady Horlick'; the blue, scented *R.* 'Songbird'; *R.* 'Glory of Athlone' (a cross between *R.* 'Earl of Athlone' and *R.* 'Glory of Leonardslee'); and some that were never properly named, such as one Horlick called the 'Three Cs' (a cross between *R. concinnum*, *R. concatenans* and *R. cinnabarinum*).

When Horlick came to Gigha, it was the perfect place to set out and expand his collection by carving out niches in the woodland to fill with new plants – the main problem was always the threat of the invasive *R. ponticum*, which would overwhelm the new plants if not kept in check. He exchanged rhododendrons with many memorable gardens within and beyond Scotland, including The Savill Garden (now part of Windsor Park) and Bodnant (in North Wales).

In 1972, a new species of tender pink rhododendron, initially collected by Frank Kingdon-Ward in the 1930s, was rediscovered in the collection at the Royal Botanic Garden Edinburgh, where it had remained unnamed. It was also the year that Horlick died, and so *R. horlickianum* was the name given to this special specimen, which can still be seen in the Royal Botanic Garden Edinburgh glasshouses.

Rhododendron 'Glory of Athlone'

Rhododendron 'Elsie Watson'

Rhododendron 'Mrs James Horlick'

Rhododendron 'Gigha Gem'

propagating and maintaining the living plants in good order. He wanted to ensure that, after his death, the fund was used to encourage the public to enjoy the garden in every possible way and to guard against the collection having to be removed from the Isle of Gigha. Horlick was awarded the Victoria Medal of Honour by the RHS in 1963, for his work on rhododendron breeding and education.

A NEW DAWN

For the people of Gigha, Achamore Gardens are not a separate entity - they are part of what makes Gigha special and are a huge part of their heritage and history. Many of the families have memories of growing up there, playing there and working there. There is a general feeling that Achamore is not just 'Horlick's Garden' - it is a central part of the island's history and of the story of the people. But the days when there were up to fifty workers on the estate is in the past; a new model has to be found - one that will work for the future.

Horlick died in 1972, while Malcolm Allan had died two years earlier. Peter Clough (who had also worked at Tresco; see page 29), took over the post of head gardener from 1970 to 1974. Over the following three decades, Gigha changed hands several times with consequent variable attention being paid to the gardens. Then, in March 2002, the 170 islanders were successful in a community buyout of the Isle of Gigha. Shortly afterwards, the community had to sell Achamore House to pay back some of the loans. Its gardens, however, remained in the community's care - an awkward arrangement for both the subsequent house owners and the other islanders.

The Isle of Gigha Heritage Trust (IGHT) tried to keep the gardens going with a much-reduced staff. Micropropagation of the important rhododendrons was not a big success, while the logistics of trying to bring in mulch or gravel by ferry, for example, proved prohibitively expensive. Since 2017, however, new fund-raising activity has enabled the IGHT to lead the restoration of the gardens and facilitate participation, engagement and regeneration. It hopes to reunite the house with its garden to make a centre where environmental, horticultural and community projects can take place.

There are huge financial and practical challenges for these gardens. The island has its own natural springs and two of them emerge in the gardens. When rainfall is heavy, the lower parts of the gardens flood, creating perfect conditions for sheets of primulas and bog plants, but putting the other plants at risk. The other major challenge is just the sheer number of trees outgrowing their allotted space. The stands planted fifty years earlier for shelter - sycamores (*Acer pseudoplatanus*), birch (*Betula*), elms (*Ulmus*) and horse chestnuts (*Aesculus hippocastanum*) - have turned into impenetrable thickets, obscuring the views. This presents great opportunities for woodland wildlife education, but also threatens some rare trees and shrubs - a balance that will have to be carefully handled. Yet, every challenge could offer students and special interest groups a chance to put their theories into practice in an unrivalled setting - and provide work and volunteering opportunities on the island.

That new model is in its infancy; it may well serve as a framework for other estates where the horticultural heritage needs protection. Sustainable is a word often used carelessly, but it is taken hugely seriously at Achamore Gardens, where resources are finite and materials expensive. Horlick never finished his gardens, and they are still a work in progress. When the residents succeeded in buying their own island, they described the new era in Gaelic as *Latha Ghiogha* (a new dawn). This could apply equally to the future of Achamore House and its gardens.

OPPOSITE CLOCKWISE FROM TOP LEFT: The 0.8-hectare/2-acre walled garden at Achamore; bluebells colonize the woodland; the original carriageway up to the house; one of the hundreds of clearings made by James Horlick for his plant collections; laburnums in the walled garden.

ANGLESEY: YNYS MÔN

THE ISLE OF ANGLESEY is Wales's largest island and the seventh largest in the British Isles. Until Thomas Telford completed his suspension bridge in 1826, followed in 1850 by Robert Stephenson's rail bridge, the only access for goods or people was by ferry across the short, but notoriously dangerous, Menai Strait.

A popular holiday destination for the urban population, Anglesey has always been valued for its 'wildness' - most of the coastline is designated as an Area of Outstanding Natural Beauty (AONB). It is also geologically special, as demonstrated by the fact that it is a Unesco Global Geopark (GeoMôn) in recognition of its complex layers of rock strata, much of which is visible from the coastal path. It is mainly low-lying, with no hills above 220m/722ft, and gives some of the best views of the Snowdonia mountain range on the mainland - that is, when the mist clears. Anglesey has high humidity (above 75 per cent for most of the year) and 60-70 per cent cloud cover. It is rarely cold, though - almost never dipping below 5°C/41°F - and the warming influence of the sea has historically made the island a good place to make gardens.

Most visitors will make first for Plas Newydd, the seat of the marquesses of Anglesey. The house with its Rex Whistler connections and Humphry Repton landscape is well worth visiting. However, just a few kilometres along the coast there is less well-known garden, tucked away between Menai Bridge and Beaumaris, in the coastal settlement of Cadnant.

PREVIOUS PAGES: The Tŵr Mawr beacon is a waymarker for walkers taking the 200-kilometre/124-mile coastal path around the island.
LEFT: The ancient village of Cadnant marks one of the narrowest crossing points of the Menai Strait.

Plas Cadnant

Buying the 81-hectare/200-acre Plas Cadnant estate was a true case of heart over head for forty-five-year-old dairy farmer Anthony Tavernor, who discovered the overgrown grounds and dilapidated sixteenth-century farm in 1996. It turned out to be just the project he had been looking for - a magical combination of landscape, history, architecture and gardens - and one that would absorb him for the next two decades.

At first, the gardens showed little promise or even any evidence of previous horticulture. Fully grown trees filled the old walled garden while the lower ravine and river were evident only from the sound of crashing water and not even remotely approachable in person through the canopy of *Rhododendron ponticum* and self-seeded cherry laurels (*Prunus laurocerasus*).

The first stage was to rescue the outbuildings and gardener's cottage, using traditional techniques and materials, to create holiday accommodation that would bring income. Work started on restoring the gardens and grounds in 1997, and little by little Tavernor and a team of friends and volunteers uncovered not one but three separate gardens: the walled garden with its curved profile walls; an upper woodland garden; and the secret valley garden with its river and waterfall.

Like the garden itself, the story of Plas Cadnant has unfolded gradually. The walled garden turned out to have medieval origins, but landscaping really began in 1804 when John Price, a local farmer, married an heiress - thus joining their assets: the combined area was in excess of 1,200 hectares/3,000 acres. This marriage created the two prerequisites for a garden of note - money and land - and enabled the Price family to place their house and garden within the fashionable Picturesque movement of art, architecture and design.

The Prices became stewards to the marquesses of Anglesey at Plas Newydd, and the development of Plas Cadnant probably owes a lot to the influence of the parkland there, where Repton had worked. The nineteenth-century interpretation of the

From the house, the gardens slope down to the mouth of the Afon (river) Cadnant and give views towards Snowdonia.

Picturesque put emphasis on natural features, enhancing the inherent beauty of a landscape and creating an experience when you walked around of being 'surprised'. Price took the natural river and mill pool at the bottom of the valley (once used to power woollen mills) and turned it into his own vision of paradise, using both native and exotic shrubs, and creating walkways, streams and waterfalls. The functional kitchen garden was made to look more aesthetically pleasing, and areas were planted around the house to frame the views.

It is easy to forget that all this landscaping was done at a time when everything would have arrived by boat across the Menai Strait - although labour was plentiful and cheap. Sadly, it was the waters of the Strait that later contributed to the demise of the Prices - John Price's grandson was drowned while out fishing, and a series of other family problems meant that the estate began a slow decline.

Plas Cadnant certainly has echoes of the Lost Gardens of Heligan in Cornwall. Both estates lost many working men and women to the First World War, and Plas Cadnant struggled on until 1928, when it was divided and sold off in lots. The penultimate owner, Elizabeth Fanning-Evans, was a cousin of the Tremaynes of Heligan and developed areas of the gardens in the 1940s. She was a keen gardener but, inevitably, the cultivated area dwindled until she could manage only a small corner of the walled garden. That too would soon disappear under a canopy of self-sown trees and shrubs.

A paved garden has been planted with culinary herbs beside the old dairy, left, now restored as accommodation.

A GENTLE RENAISSANCE

An interesting history is one thing, but deciding how to restore and rebuild a garden in the here and now is something different altogether. For twenty years, this was Tavernor's obsession and along with willing friends and helpers he worked his way through the dense wood to find what was left of this historic landscape. Carefully and meticulously, three separate gardens were uncovered - but there were no botanical treasures. Using the original framework, the current planting was set out from scratch and is the more remarkable for that.

As the old farm buildings were restored, their courtyards were planted up with formal box (*Buxus*) hedging and herbs. In the walled garden, it would have been impossible to return to full vegetable production so new fruit trees were planted, Elizabeth Fanning-Evans' 'corner' was restored, and a small vegetable garden was stocked by the award-winning vegetable growers Medwyns of Anglesey. The raised border that was originally a covered terrace for growing early vegetables has been given a bold planting scheme, with attention paid to foliage colour and form. Most of the walled garden remains as open lawn, with clipped pyramid yews (*Taxus*) bringing geometric form. New terraces have been built above the garden to deal with the slopes and to give good views over the walled gardens - one of these terraces has been filled with a double herbaceous border.

BELOW: Former working yards at Plas Cadnant have been transformed with box hedging and clipped topiary.
FOLLOWING PAGES: Below the walled garden with its formal pool is the valley where the Afon Cadnant meets the Menai Strait.

ABOVE: The double herbaceous border on the raised terrace is divided into bays punctuated by fastigiate yews.
OPPOSITE: A lightly scented rambler, *Rosa* 'Phyllis Bide', frames the entrance to the double herbaceous border.

The double herbaceous border was not a feature of the original garden, but has developed over a decade or more into an important component, designed to unfold through the seasons. The space was divided into compartments by yew buttresses shaped to reflect the catenary curves on Telford's Suspension Bridge. By summer, however, the buttresses all but disappear beneath the tiers of planting, influenced by the plantsman Graham Stuart Thomas. These consist of a chevron pattern that begins with blue and yellow at the top end (where visitors normally approach) through to reds, pinks and purple towards the far end. Along the length of the border, Tavernor has set eight upright yews (*Taxus baccata* 'Fastigiata Robusta') - four on each side - to break up the flow. The blues and purples are provided first by *Allium hollandicum* 'Purple Sensation' and then by tall, blue *Campanula lactiflora* 'Pritchard's Variety', while the blocks of pink and red belong to *Persicaria amplexicaulis* and to the deepening flower heads of sedums (*Hylotelephium*). Height is added by *Eupatorium purpureum* while asters and dahlias continue the display into autumn.

Although the structure of the border is formal, which ensures it looks good even when the planting is less full, the style is relaxed and includes hardy geraniums and perennial foxgloves (*Digitalis grandiflora*), which enjoy the open position. As a whole, the double border makes a good contrast to the planting of the upper and lower valleys, which have more shade, moving water and rocky outcrops.

ABOVE: Before restoration began, the 0.8-hectare/2-acre walled garden had disappeared under a 'forest' of self-seeded sycamores (*Acer pseudoplatanus*) and *Rhododendron ponticum*.

RIGHT: As it would have been impossible to restore the walled garden to full production, only a small section was cleared and this is now kept for vegetables and cutting flowers – here sweet peas (*Lathyrus odoratus*).

ABOVE: The wall beyond the pool has been deliberately curved to reflect the engineering prowess of Thomas Telford's suspension bridge just a few kilometres from the garden.

LEFT: To create structure and form in the lawned garden, the path towards the pool is flanked by twenty yew pyramids, kept sharply clipped.

The cool, shady conditions of the upper valley allow candelabra primulas, arum lilies (*Zantedeschia aethiopica*) and soft shield ferns (*Polystichum setiferum*) to thrive.

The upper valley begins its show in late winter with snowdrops (*Galanthus*), through primulas and azaleas in spring to hydrangeas in late summer. During the restoration, this area was replanted and new, sinuous paths laid out, echoing its Picturesque origins in the early nineteenth century. An archway of Japanese snowbell (*Styrax japonica*) marks the entrance to the lower valley, which is now a masterpiece of exotic and native planting beneath mature trees.

This woodland garden, once hidden under cherry laurels and brambles, is now a network of steps and paths that lead the visitor to explore dells of bluebells and ferns in spring, after which they emerge by the waterfall. At the lowest point, where the Prices had engineered the waters of the Afon Cadnant, an impressive piece of quartz rock was recently discovered - it had been hidden by brambles but had always been intended to be seen and to bring a sense of theatre to this part of the garden. Now Himalayan lilies (see opposite) as well as shade-loving royal ferns (*Osmunda regalis*), shield ferns (*Polystichum*) and buckler ferns (*Dryopteris*) enhance this landscape of rocks and water.

The day came when Tavernor knew that to secure the future of Plas Cadnant it must be opened to the public and shared with others. The discussion about what to call it began. It was a truly 'lost' garden that was found, but they had no wish to copy Heligan. In the end, they chose the Hidden Gardens of Plas Cadnant, which describes

HIMALAYAN LILY

The largest of all lilies, Himalayan lily (*Cardiocrinum giganteum*) was collected in the Himalayas and brought to Europe in the 1850s by, among others, the Lobb brothers of the Veitch nursery in London's Chelsea and in Devon. After years of plant hunting (including collecting the Himalayan lily in the foothills of Nepal), Thomas Lobb lost his leg from exposure on an expedition to the Philippines, and never quite attained the fame of his older brother William.

Thomas's specimen was shown at the Royal Horticultural Society show in Chiswick, London in 1853 (the forerunner of RHS Chelsea Flower Show), although, in fact, a Himalayan lily had been exhibited in Edinburgh a year earlier, albeit one grown from seed, not collected as a growing plant. Such was the competition for bringing these choice plants back to British gardens that people would risk their lives and their livelihoods for the accolade.

Apart from its stature (reaching 2–4m/7–13ft, depending on conditions), the attraction of the Himalayan lily is the beautiful pale flowers, which are strongly scented. It is not, however, happy everywhere; it needs cool, shady conditions in summer and rich, fertile soil with plenty of humus. It is tolerant of cold winters, and even if temperatures drop to –10°C/14°F the bulbous part underground will probably survive. Although the first bulbs took seven years to bloom at Plas Cadnant, the colony is now well established and increasing. Their flowers appear from early summer, releasing their scent across the lower valley.

Cardiocrinum giganteum

not only its geographical situation, invisible from the Menai Strait, but also the fact that it has kept its secrets buried for the best part of a century.

Plas Cadnant's position, in a deep, south-east-facing valley, has been both its blessing and its misfortune. On 26 December 2015, the land above, saturated with continuous heavy rain, unloaded water into the Cadnant valley. The garden filled like a reservoir, the weight of water finally breaking through the lower walls and pushing the newly restored stonework 500 metres/550 yards down into the river below.

Television coverage of the disaster drew people in from far and wide, and within a year the walls had been repaired and the garden was thriving again. By attracting funding and by employing local people, Tavernor has put Plas Cadnant on to a sustainable footing and safeguarded it for the future. Yet this is still not a 'public' garden in any sense of the word. It is a personal garden with great heart . . . that also warmly welcomes visitors.

OPPOSITE: The pool at the bottom of the lower valley was transformed from a former mill pond, used when Cadnant had a thriving woollen industry.
BELOW LEFT: This huge piece of natural rock – part of the original Picturesque landscape – was only recently discovered.
BELOW RIGHT: Natural streams were manipulated to enhance the rugged landscape at Plas Cadnant.

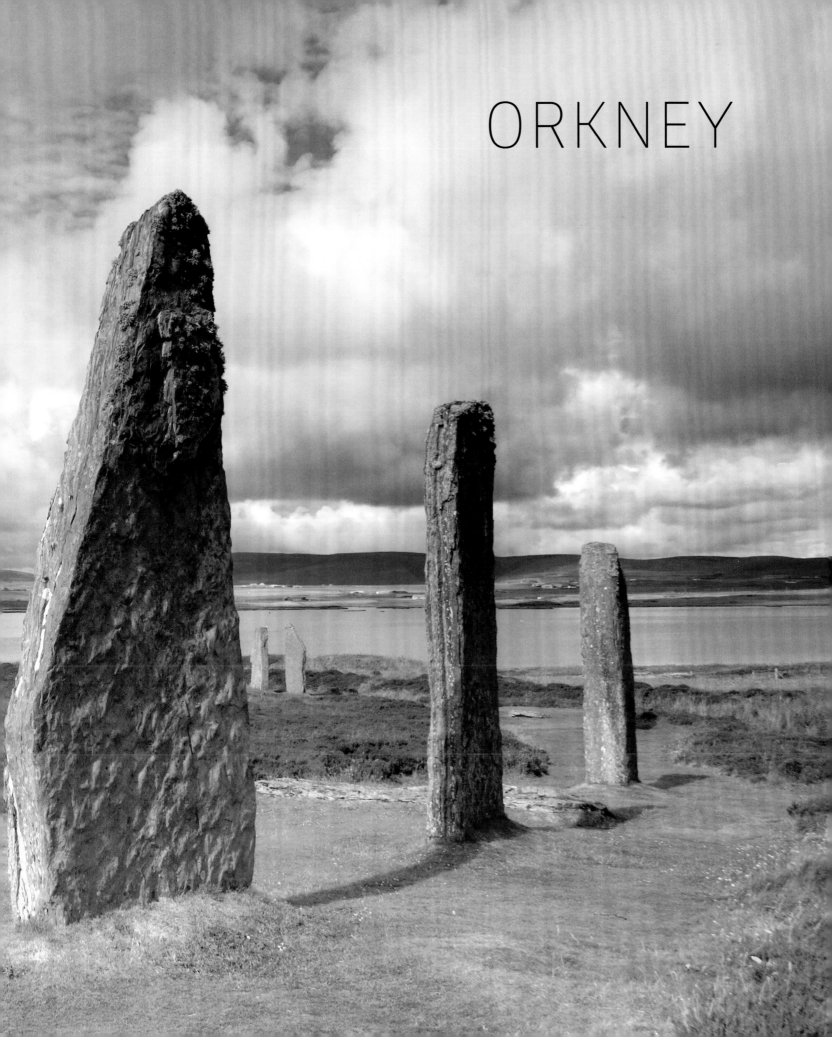

ORKNEY

BEYOND THE NORTHERNMOST POINT of the British mainland lie the sixty or more islands that make up Orkney, one of the most archaeologically vibrant places in Europe. The islands have been inhabited for ten thousand years, with most of the those people living on Mainland (from the Norse *Meginland*), South Ronaldsay, Burra or Hoy, or on one of the outer islands: Eday, North Ronaldsay, Shapinsay, Sanday, Rousay, Egilsay, Stronsay, Westray and Papa Westray.

In terms of its culture - music, literature, art and archaeology - Orkney is often at the heart of things, and this applies to its gardens, too. The impracticality of adapting any particular style of British or European garden to their local conditions has meant that Orcadians have carved a horticultural niche of their own.

Because of its weather, this is no place for the frail or faint-hearted. The wind is an ever-present fact of life, but rainfall is not excessive (900-1,500mm/35-60in), winters are mild and summers cool. The long day length in summer means growth is packed into a mere five months, from late spring to early autumn, and it is this window of opportunity - and perhaps the thought of the long, dark winters - that spurs Orkney gardeners to be so fearless.

PREVIOUS PAGES: The Ring of Brodgar is part of a string of Neolithic sites along the narrow isthmus known as the Ness of Brodgar, dating to at least 3000 BC.
LEFT: Westray, with its nineteenth-century lighthouse, is home to around 600 people - and hundreds of thousands of seabirds.

The Quoy of Houton
MAINLAND

The week before the June 2017 opening of Caroline and Kevin Critchlow's garden near Orphir, overlooking Scapa Flow, the gales came in from the north-west. Three days of 80-96km/h/50-6omph winds tore through the garden, decimating the plants. That is the reality of gardening on Orkney, but particularly for gardeners with a sea view.

Undeterred, Caroline removed four barrowloads of damaged plants and replaced them with her 'back up' stocks from the cold frame, and local nurseries also helped to fill the gaps. She believes there are only two ways to garden in Orkney: you either plant shelter belts of trees and garden behind this protection, or else - as at the Quoy of Houton - you keep the garden exposed so that you retain the sea view, and accept that the turnover of plants may be huge.

At the Quoy, the eighteenth-century walls of what had been the laird's house enclosed a plot that had never been gardened before the Critchlows arrived here

OPPOSITE: The garden at the Quoy faces directly out to Scapa Flow.
BELOW: Ornamentation is restricted to sturdy, blue-painted seats and obelisks, while the flagpole bearing the flag of Orkney is the only really tall feature in the garden.
FOLLOWING PAGES: The garden now includes an oval lawn, a rill, shrubs and herbaceous planting, with plenty of places to sit and take in the view.

in 2007. The couple had honeymooned on Orkney and romantically decided to live there for the rest of their lives. They designed the garden in one go, using Kevin Critchlow's skill as a farmer and drystone waller. They brought in 100 tonnes of dry stone, and set a rectangular rill in the centre of the garden, to draw your eye towards the view over the water.

MARINE LIFE

The rill has been divided into two by a central bridge, making one area for fish and another for wildlife. The garden gate is not to stop deer or rabbits, but to shut out the otters that come up from the shore to take the fish if given the opportunity. The water plants have to be pinned to the bottom with metal stakes to stop them being thrown out of the water by the gales. Unlike many Scottish gardens, moisture-loving primulas are not naturally happy here but are being persevered with around the edges.

The planting beds were placed against the walls for protection and the earth removed from the building of the rill was used to create raised beds, which give good drainage for the plants on these north- and south-facing aspects. The garden began with what can loosely be described as 'Orkney plants' - those that grow easily there including willows (*Salix*), lady's mantle (*Alchemilla mollis*), crocosmias, libertias, common bistorts (*Persicaria bistorta*), dusky cranesbills (*Geranium phaeum*) (in the shadier spots) and *G.* 'Johnson's Blue' (in the sun), as well as some of the Orkney geraniums bred by local farmer Alan Bremner - the toughest of these, according to Caroline, are *G.* Patricia and *G.* × *cantabrigiense* 'St Ola'. She hopes gradually to build up a National Collection.

From these basics, a planting evolved that reflects both the sea and the sky, with lots of blues interspersed with spots of other colours to break it up. Caroline tried different cultivars of the island stalwarts, such as *Persicaria amplexicaulis* 'Rosea' and *Potentilla thurberi* 'Monarch's Velvet', which are doing well.

Just because something is easy to grow and looks at home in a border doesn't mean a gardener will be content. Caroline wanted to grow things that would be in complete contrast to the surrounding landscape, so the garden is also full of fragrant roses and Gertrude Jekyll-inspired corners, as well as tall plants such as alliums, lupins and foxgloves, which are regularly and inevitably cut down by the wind - and cheerfully replanted. Even the escallonias - sturdy hedging elsewhere on Orkney - lose their leaves in winter in this garden. The only way to achieve good planting has been to place green windbreak mesh panels diagonally along the length of the raised beds to mitigate the effects of the winds.

NATURAL CONDITIONS

The soil at the Quoy is naturally light and sandy, and the wind also strips it of moisture, meaning that, despite the relatively high rainfall, whenever winds are forecast watering is carried out assiduously. The combination of salt and rain leaches fertilizers from the lawn, too, leaving it pale and yellowing after a storm, so keeping it looking green is an ongoing struggle.

Islanders tend to acquire plants from each other, either by informal swapping or supporting one of the several nurseries on the island. Most plants are raised outdoors and are therefore fit for purpose; the use of a greenhouse would be counterproductive as the plants would be too tender for Orcadian conditions.

Caroline is something of a local gardening celebrity with her regular contributions to Radio Orkney and *The Beechgrove Garden* - Scotland's longest-running gardening TV show. Yet the garden at the Quoy of Houton might never have been opened to the public had not Kevin Critchlow been diagnosed with a brain tumour in 2013. With no facilities on the island, Kevin was treated at the Neuro Ward at Aberdeen Royal Infirmary (ARI). Caroline decided to give something back by opening the garden to raise money for the Friends of the Neuro Ward, which she founded. She also initiated the Orkney Garden Trail, which gives access in June and July every other year to some twenty-eight gardens across Orkney, in aid of charity. Kevin has recovered and runs drystone-walling courses, and the couple have converted their barns into holiday accommodation.

Great things happen under difficult circumstances. Caroline has galvanized latent gardeners throughout the islands to be proud of their achievements and to share these with the wider public, who are no longer amazed by the fact that creating gardens is an art that Orkney also excels at.

OPPOSITE CLOCKWISE FROM TOP LEFT: The Quoy of Houton; the terraces and rill were made from Orkney flagstone; *Miscanthus sinensis* 'Variegatus' and hardy geraniums in the raised beds; planting is kept low so as not to spoil the view; stone sphere by Kevin Critchlow; white foxgloves (*Digitalis purpurea* f. *albiflora*) and *Thalictrum aquilegiifolium*.

Fiddlers Green
SOUTH RONALDSAY

In the village of Herston close to St Margaret's Hope, where the ferry from Caithness docks, there is a row of old herring fishermen's cottages built in the 1860s. Originally, all the cottages had long strips of almost 0.4 hectares/1 acre of land running behind the house to keep a cow and grow vegetables. One of them - Fiddlers Green - is home to Mike and Sue Palmer, who, as at the Quoy of Houton (see page 78), garden 'to the view'.

The challenges here are equally breathtaking - the garden lies at the bottom of a slope and sits on top of clay (only a spade's depth down), making it rather soggy. At the back, water runs into the garden, so a lawn is out of the question, but the Palmers manage to grow vegetables in raised beds. At the front they make the best of the space with a vibrant gravel garden.

Because the winter gales and accompanying salt spray regularly hit the front garden, the gravel area is planted with mainly herbaceous perennials: hardy geraniums, Jacob's ladder (*Polemonium*), dicentras, valerian (*Centranthus*), astrantias and various campanulas. The Palmers say it is always such a relief to see them coming into growth again in spring. Spring and summer bulbs fill the gaps alongside plenty of self-seeders: sisyrinchiums, poppies (*Papaver*), nasturtiums (*Tropaeolum*) and *Cerinthe major*, which are easy to pull out of the gravel if they seed inappropriately.

The wind has other consequences, too - 30 knots (or 56km/h/35mph) is considered 'normal' and twice this force is frequent - so seating in the garden must be sturdy, made of heavy wood or stone that won't blow away. The growing season is short - from late spring to early autumn. Late spring can be glorious but there is also the Gabs of May, which is a stormy period at the beginning of the month bringing rain and winds - sometimes referred to as the lambing wind. Late summer can also be wet and windy. By early autumn, the growing season is finished. Winter here is never very cold, with no prolonged frosts or snow, but the wind-chill factor can keep the temperature down. And then there are the dark nights . . .

None of this deters gardeners like those at Herston, who open their gardens for charity. They enjoy the plus points: the amazing view; the long day length in summer; and most of them collect seaweed from their own shoreline frontage and add it to the compost heap. The seaweed acts as an accelerator to speed up the composting process, rotting the other materials down more quickly.

RICHES OF THE SEA

Traditionally, Orcadians, along with many other Scottish islanders, have turned to seaweed as a free and readily available way to improve soil structure and add nutrients. However, this small-scale, household use was overtaken by commercial collection and burning, to produce kelp - a concentrated form of alkali used in the making of glass and soap. This was part of the general 'improvements' of the second half of the eighteenth and early nineteenth century, and at one time thousands of men, women and children were employed to cut the seaweed, dry it over low stone walls and then tend the burning kilns on the beach. By the early twentieth century, kelp production was finished, but the tradition of collecting seaweed for gardens has never quite vanished.

The garden at Fiddlers Green runs down to the shore and is designed for spring and summer impact, with lupins, aquilegias and Jacob's ladder giving a cottage-garden feel to the planting.

Kierfiold House

MAINLAND

Kierfiold House stands on its own on the northern slope above Loch Skaill in the borough of Sandwick on western Mainland. It was originally intended as the dower house for Skaill House (best known for the discovery of the Neolithic houses on its shoreline at Skara Brae). However, Kierfiold was instead used by the local laird for several decades, with the result that there has been a garden at Kierfiold since 1852.

The house and 1-hectare/2.5-acre plot was bought by Fiona and Euan Smith in 2005. Two of the previous owners had made an impact on the garden: the Scotts, who lived there from the 1930s; and John and Pauline Munro, from the 1990s. John Munro was a keen gardener and hardy geranium enthusiast, but there were limited written records about the garden, leaving Fiona Smith – who had only ever gardened on a much smaller scale – to make what she could of the densely planted plot.

OPPOSITE: Long mown grass paths lead the eye down the long border and out to the hills of Harray beyond.
BELOW: Kierfiold House above Loch Skaill is an unusual place to find a well-maintained, plant-filled garden.
FOLLOWING PAGES: Not a square centimetre of ground is left unplanted, as low-growing herbaceous perennials compete for space.

The main focus has been the 0.2-hectare/½-acre walled garden at the front of the house, which lies on a gentle slope and faces south-east towards the hills of Harray. So far, more than a hundred different hardy geraniums have been identified in the garden and Fiona has become, de facto, a very knowledgeable enthusiast who is expanding the collection.

GARDENS WITHIN GARDENS

Protection from the wind on this exposed site has been crucial. The walls themselves provide the first line of defence, enhanced at the bottom of the slope and to the south side by a line of what are known on Orkney as 'sacrificial' trees - sycamore (*Acer pseudoplatanus*) - which grow sturdy and gnarled, if not tall. Within the walls, the garden is made up of compartments, created by *Fuchsia magellanica*, *Olearia traversii* and *Escallonia rubra* var. *macrantha* hedging or by low, stone walls, making the journey through the space intriguing. Because of these sheltering hedges and walls, the garden at Kierfield House can support herbaceous planting, and as many choice plants as possible are packed into the beds, which are separated only by tiny stone paths and stepping stones for access. Here the planting includes crocosmias, Jacob's ladder (*Polemonium caeruleum*), astilbes, libertias, astrantias and the architectural New Zealand flax (*Phormium tenax*).

There are other 'gardens within gardens' including an alpine area and a small enclosed lawn. At the top of the garden, another fuchsia hedge above the wall separates the terrace from the main garden and adds a line of extra protection for the house. Below it, a border of Japanese anemones (*Anemone × hybrida*) and lady's mantle (*Alchemilla mollis*) thrive in the shade. The soil is mainly sandy, although there are pockets of clay. Water percolates through the ground, making it dry

Narrow stone paths wind between the dense herbaceous planting in the sloping area of garden in front of Kierfield House.

HARDY GERANIUMS ON ORKNEY

The author and plantswoman Margery Fish famously wrote: 'When in doubt, plant a geranium.' Interest in hardy geraniums, also known as cranesbills, as reliable, hardy garden plants boomed in the 1970s, and there are now 110 species and 600 cultivars grown in British gardens. It is the sheer range of flower shapes, colour variations and uses in the garden – as ground cover, border plants and alpines – that excites geranium growers.

Like a wave, this interest in geraniums spread even to Orkney, where one farmer has spent his life breeding these plants. Alan Bremner, of St Ola, a parish near Kirkwall, deliberately crossed different species and produced what are known as Orkney geraniums. These include well-known ones such as *G.* Patricia – officially *G.* Patricia ('Brempat') – with its black eye, a cross between *G. endressii* and *G. psilostemon*; and many that have local connections such the white-flowered *G.* x *cantabrigiense*
'St Ola' and pink *G.* x *c.* 'Westray' named after the Orkney island where Bremner's father came from. 'Westray' provides a compact evergreen mat with small leaves; it is good for edging and for growing under deciduous trees as it tolerates some shade. Others have names that really reflect the character of Orkney, and people grow them for that reason. These include bronze-leaved *G.* x *antipodeum* 'Sea Spray' and *G.* 'Storm Chaser', as well as the self-explanatory *G.* 'Orkney Pink' and *G.* 'Orkney Blue'.

Most Orkney gardeners grow a large range of hardy geraniums, which seem to tolerate anything the weather can throw at them. *Geranium* x *magnificum* can be seen all over the islands, as can *G.* x *oxonianum* 'A.T. Johnson' and many different species geraniums. Interestingly, it is some of the Orkney-bred geraniums that are more of a challenge here, but gardeners such as the ones in this chapter are continuing to safeguard this fascinating plant heritage.

G. orientalitibeticum

G. Patricia ('Brempat')

G. x magnificum

G. x oxonianum 'A.T. Johnson'

G. clarkei 'Kashmir White'

G. nodosum

G. pratense var. pratense f. albiflorum

ABOVE: A clump of *Gladiolus communis* subsp. *byzantinus* marks the end of the long border. The southern boundary is protected from the wind by a line of sycamore trees.

RIGHT: Kierfiold's resident cat, Elan, is from the island of Hoy, where a genetic trait has led to cats with unusual tails - Elan's is short, rather like a Manx cat.

ABOVE: The small alpine garden is protected by low stone walls and is home to a small collection of Orkney geraniums and other alpine plants. The pink geranium on the wall is G. × *cantabrigiense* 'Westray', which is named after one of the Orkney islands.

LEFT: The citrus-yellow flowers of lady's mantle contrast with the vibrant pink gladioli.

overall, although it is slightly damper at the lower end, where the gunnera thrives.

The Smiths have altered the layout of the Kierfiold House garden relatively little, but have added seating areas, sheltered by shrubs and hedging. Two wide herbaceous borders on either side of the central enclosure are edged with grass paths that take the eye down towards the end of the garden. The borders are planted with more geraniums, the silver- or cream-striped sedge *Carex morrowii*, *Lysimachia punctata*, monkshood (*Aconitum napellus*), globe thistles (*Echinops*) and poppies (*Papaver*), with honeysuckles (*Lonicera*) against the walls. Self-seeded *Gladiolus communis* subsp. *byzantinus* adds a flash of colour in the short summer season. Fiona's philosophy is not to fight nature, but to let such plants self-seed and run together as they see fit; she acts only as mediator, to control some of the more aggressive plants and to give the less robust ones a chance.

Considering the northerly latitude of Orkney (approximately the same as Newfoundland and Labrador and just 80 kilometres/50 miles south of Greenland) there are plants that thrive here year-round because of the almost frost-free winters; these include *Fascicularia bicolor* and *Osteospermum* 'Pink Whirls'.

The previous owner of Kierfiold House, John Munro, moved to the mainland of Scotland but continues to bring cuttings for Fiona to pot on and add to Kierfiold's collection. In the coming years, her focus is to extend the alpines and build up the Orkney geraniums (see page 91), as well as add more late-flowering geraniums, which will extend the season of the garden. Many of the less-hardy geraniums will overwinter better in Orkney than in British gardens farther south, and Fiona enjoys contributing to social media with stories of her successes. Kierfiold House is a surprising garden with hidden depths and one that defies its location.

OPPOSITE: Bronze-leaved rodgersia, yellow loosestrife (*Lysimachia*) and *Geranium clarkei* 'Kashmir Purple' have all proved themselves hardy in the borders at Kierfiold House.
BELOW: On the opposite side of the garden, oriental poppies (*Papaver orientale*) make an impact among the aruncus and hostas.

CLOSE TO THE COAST of northern France, but enjoying a special status as Crown Dependencies of the UK, the Channel Islands (Îles de la Manche) are very much part of the British Isles. They consist of two Bailiwicks (Guernsey and Jersey), which in the case of Guernsey, includes the islands of Alderney, Sark and Herm.

Historically, the islands belonged to the Duchy of Normandy, though that claim was settled in 1259 under Henry III of England. However, they were never absorbed into England, Great Britain or the UK, and they retain their particular status with different legal and tax systems. The language spoken is largely English, although there are some ancient Norman dialects, and French place names are prevalent.

The Channel Islands were the only British territories occupied by the Germans in the Second World War, and such a history proves a big draw for visitors. The other attraction of the islands is their kilometres of coastline, high sunshine levels and mild climate - a combination that has made the islands a place to go and see gardens and flowers.

GUERNSEY

This island has a rich history of horticultural production, particularly of flowers, tomatoes and grapes, which has left a legacy that pervades the island. Gardeners also know Guernsey as the home of clematis - the Raymond Evison Clematis nursery has been based there for more than thirty years and provides huge numbers of new clematis varieties worldwide. The long growing season and high light levels mean that propagation can go on for nine months of the year, and this gives growers there a head start over the competition on mainland Britain. In addition, Guernsey has become known for cut flower production and every spring and autumn growers and gardeners come together for flower festivals.

PREVIOUS PAGES: Foxgloves (*Digitalis purpurea*) grow wild on the shores of Jersey, another of the Channel Islands.
RIGHT: On the outskirts of St Peter Port, the gardens at Fermain Valley Hotel have been cleverly planted to merge into the natural vegetation.

In terms of public gardens, St Peter Port - the main population centre of Guernsey's east coast - has its well-loved Victorian park, Candie Gardens, which is a great example of the genre. However, for new styles of planting it is often tourism and hotels that are driving innovation. Just outside St Peter Port, the Fermain Valley Hotel has utilized its position in a natural valley to make gardens with lush planting that seems to go down to the shore. Private gardens have not always been such a visible part of the horticultural picture, but many are now actively promoted by Floral Guernsey, attracting tourists and locals alike to scheduled charity openings.

Guernsey has become particularly closely connected with one group of plants - the nerines. The Latin name of the red Guernsey lily, *Nerine sarniensis*, suggests that it originated on the island (*sarniensis* meaning 'from Guernsey'), but in fact it is a South African plant that hails from a coastal climate of wet winters and dry summers. It travelled to Europe in the early seventeenth century. One story dates its introduction to a shipwreck, whereas another claims it was brought in by

a political prisoner during the English Civil War of 1642-51, when Guernsey sided with the Parliamentarians. Either way, its association with the island dates back centuries.

Hybridization began in earnest in the late nineteenth and early twentieth centuries - and the list of famous horticulturalists who bred from the Guernsey lily include Max Leichtlin of Baden Baden, Henry John Elwes of Colesbourne in Gloucestershire and Lionel de Rothschild of Exbury. The oldest hybrid on Guernsey is probably the orange one known as *N.* × *versicolor* 'Mansellii', which dates back to 1875.

Guernsey lilies flower from late summer through to early winter. Even in Guernsey, which is usually frost-free, they are grown in a greenhouse to ensure good flowering.

Every October, the town of St Peter Port on Guernsey hosts a nerine festival, when members of the Plant Heritage Group bring together hundreds of different species and cultivars. These vary in colour from deep red, through oranges, pinks and white, to make a spectacular display in the Victorian greenhouses at Candie Gardens.

OPPOSITE: The Victorian Candie Gardens are the focus of Guernsey's regular flower festivals.

ABOVE: The Guernsey lily (*Nerine sarniensis*) is grown under glass in pots and as a cut flower.

LEFT: The glasshouses at Candie Park were built in 1793 and are among the oldest surviving examples in the British Isles.

La Bigoterie
GUERNSEY

One of several gardens that open for charity on Guernsey is La Bigoterie, situated high above St Peter Port. The oldest part of the house was built in the eighteenth century. The current owners, Huw and Sarah Evans, came to La Bigoterie in 2007, having been won over by its position and also by the possibilities of making a garden on the terraces, looking out across the harbour to the islands of Sark and Herm.

Their previous adventures in gardening had been on a grand scale; 10 hectares/25 acres outside Maidstone in Kent, designed by the late Anthony du Gard Pasley, which eventually opened under the National Garden Scheme.

The Evans family had greatly enjoyed the construction of the Kent garden and the subsequent planting. However, over time, they found the maintenance of such a large garden a huge undertaking. So, when they decided to move full-time to Guernsey, uppermost in their minds was making a garden that they would be able to maintain themselves.

As it happened, La Bigoterie had 0.2 hectares/½ acre of land, but not really a 'garden'. The terraces were grassy and full of ivy and Spanish bluebells, the seating areas were non-existent and there was no planting of any significance. But there were a couple of fruit trees on the lower terrace, substantial lime (*Tilia*) trees creating shade on the southern side, a walnut (*Juglans*) tree in the centre of the lawn and a number of mature camellias and rhododendrons, which provided some structure. In order to make the most of its potential, they invited Du Gard Pasley to visit again for a few days, and although his age and geographical distance made it impractical for him to take on the project long-term, he made an initial blueprint for the Evans family to follow.

They were much more hands-on in the creation of this garden than they were able to be in Kent and, through watching Du Gard Pasley and his team, had acquired the confidence

This private garden, overlooking Guernsey's main harbour, has a view across to the islands of Herm and Jethou and beyond to Sark.

to get started. The old walls, which divided the garden area into rooms, were renovated, while they put in a new terrace in front of the house and laid lawn around the walnut tree. They also made the pond garden, the parterre, the orchard and the vegetable garden. Sarah drew a pattern for the parterre, planted it up in box (*Buxus sempervirens*) and then set about the planting of the entire site.

On the east side, which faces the sea, and to the south she planted mixed borders of tender perennials, interspersed with shrubs and hardy perennials, particularly salvias and hardy geraniums. A few annuals are used to plug gaps in summer, and height is added for the season with cannas and grasses. The planting is changed throughout the year with biennial pale pink and white foxgloves (*Digitalis*), grown from seed and put out for spring and early summer, giving way to dahlias for a late summer hit of colour. There is no formal plan, and the planting is very much a personal selection of those plants that 'do well' there on the mildly acidic, free-draining soil. This means that *Geranium* Rozanne will mingle with cosmos, fuchsias, penstemons, sweet peas (*Lathyrus odoratus*), single and decorative dahlias, dark aeoniums and huge, striped phormiums, which grow so easily in Guernsey.

The west-facing upper terrace is given over to shrubs that need less attention: hydrangeas, camellias, the occasional rhododendron and hibiscus backed by hedges of *Olearia paniculata*, flanking steps that lead up to a shady seat with a view over the port.

On the lower terrace is a granite pond stocked with goldfish, which dart about among the water lilies (*Nymphaea*). Pink and grey granite stone, for which the Channel Islands is famous, features throughout the garden in walls and steps. However, the main paving and path material is Portland stone (from Portland Bill, near Weymouth in Dorset). The stone had long been imported to Guernsey as counter ballast, balancing the weight of ships on their return journey from the UK after delivering the granite; the most famous export of Guernsey granite was to make the steps of St Paul's Cathedral in London. Against the walls, pyracantha has been trained as geometric espaliers along wires in an experiment that is very effective.

Making the best of the various levels was a priority for this garden, which has a lawn and terrace leading down to an orchard, parterre, pool and vegetable garden.

HOME-GROWN

Growing fruit and vegetables is essential to the Evans family – their daughter is a chef by profession and access to a good range of fresh ingredients has always been a high priority. When they bought La Bigoterie the orchard already had some productive apple trees, which were augmented with a medlar (*Mespilus germanica*), a quince (*Cydonia oblonga*), two pears, greengages, cobnuts (*Corylus avellana*), a damson and a fig against the wall. Through an archway beyond the pond, the family can access the vegetable garden. This too started life as a 'field' and has been made fully functional with rectangular, timber-edged raised beds and gravel paths, which are easier to maintain than turf. Everything seems to grow well here: asparagus, climbing beans, sweetcorn, leeks, beetroot, courgettes, rhubarb and lots of leafy greens and salads such as sorrel, cavolo nero and rocket. Tomatoes are not grown in large quantities because in Guernsey they are sold everywhere as part of the Hedge Veg scheme, where small growers offer flowers and vegetables for sale from their houses and along the roadside.

For many people, Guernsey is a dream place to garden. It has no squirrels, no moles and no foxes. Recently, the garden at La Bigoterie has benefited from a borehole that provides as much water as the garden needs – something that would be impossibly expensive via the conventional water system. But nature has a way of balancing things so that gardeners don't get it all their own way, and La Bigoterie has an ongoing battle with slugs and snails.

The usual problems of island or coastal gardens have been addressed at La Bigoterie with hedges of *Olearia paniculata* and *Griselinia littoralis*, which enclose the plot; both of these plants resist the westerly winds. Salt spray is inevitable, but in winter, when the waves are crashing into the harbour walls below, the garden sits high above, and anything that might get decimated is pruned back hard to make the most of the view.

LEFT FROM TOP: *Mespilus germanica*, *Malus domestica*, runner beans 'White Lady'.
OPPOSITE CLOCKWISE FROM TOP LEFT: Borders along the sea aspect are vibrantly planted with cannas, *Dahlia* 'Bishop of Llandaff' and dark-leaved heucheras; steps lead up through hydrangeas to a Lutyens-style bench; the family's lurcher under the walnut tree; the old orchard has been restocked with young medlars, quince, pears, apples and cobnuts; the raised pond has been edged with Guernsey granite; the box parterre with an espaliered pyracantha against the wall.

Herm Island

A short boat ride by catamaran from St Peter Port on Guernsey brings you to Herm Island. Being leased from the States of Guernsey, it has a history of different tenants, including the writer Compton Mackenzie (famous for the island story *Whisky Galore*) who based his 1926 novel *Fairy Gold* on Herm. Since 2008, this island has been a privately run enterprise with hotels, beaches, self-catering cottages and a campsite as well as the gardens and landscapes that surround them. This is a holiday island, yet it is also a full-time home to around sixty people, with a one-room school for the island children.

There are no cars, no natural predators for the free-range chickens, no foxes, no moles and no badgers. Previous tenants imported game for food and sport - still most prolific are rabbits, pheasants and partridge - and there were once wallabies here, brought in by a previous tenant, and still - erroneously - spotted occasionally. The only other livestock you are likely to encounter is a herd of fifteen Guernsey calves, which are grazed on the island each summer, before being winched into a boat and returned to the main island.

Everything on Herm has to be carted off the boats and on to the island by hand at the dockside. This creates a culture of resourcefulness, where nothing goes to waste. Water is extracted from seven boreholes throughout the island, electricity is generated on the island and recycling is taken very seriously - around the harbour, old tyres and drainage pipes are adapted to make seats and plant containers.

This resourcefulness has filtered down to the team of three gardeners. Although the boreholes give a plentiful supply of water in hot, dry spells, it must never be wasted. Therefore, only the containers and any new plants get regular watering. Lawns are not mowed unnecessarily, and this helps to negate the need for watering. An old wedding marquee has been utilized as a weed-suppressing fabric under the paths, and head gardener Brett Moore refashions chopped-down trees into seats and tables. Even the ubiquitous island plant - giant tree echium (*Echium pininana*) - has a secondary use. Its thick stems are chopped down, the spikes filed off, the wood then sanded and varnished to make walking sticks, for sale in the local shop. Wooden delivery pallets are stuffed with straw held in place with wire netting to make bug hotels.

AN ISLAND GARDEN

To garden a whole island is a pretty tall order, but in this case the island is tiny, being 2.5 kilometres/1.5 miles long and 0.8 kilometres/0.5 miles wide. Everyone has more than one job so the head gardener and his second-in-command also double up as firemen and policemen and can work in the pubs and restaurants if needed. However, the gardens are high priority, considered intrinsic to the visitor experience - as well as for the staff and permanent residents.

The main gardens are around the White House, the island's forty-room hotel and its cottages. Planting varies throughout the year, but always includes colourful, Mediterranean zone species that have become synonymous with temperate islands: Norfolk Island pines (*Araucaria heterophylla*), holm oaks (*Quercus ilex*), eucalyptus, palms, agaves, agapanthus, red hot pokers (*Kniphofia*), olearias, ginger lilies (*Hedychium*), alstroemerias and phormiums. One plant in particular caused a stir in 2017 when it came into flower - *Furcraea longeava* (now *F. parmentieri*). This yucca-like plant flowers only when it reaches maturity - and then blooms twice in one year before dying.

The climate on Herm is mild in winter and warm in summer, with no frosts and only the salt winds from the Atlantic causing problems of scorching. Hedges of *Olearia traversii* and privet (*Ligustrum ovalifolium*) act as windbreaks, and the soil is light, sandy and well drained.

Wherever landscaping has been done, removing the waste materials is not an option. Herm used to have a thriving quarrying industry for granite, and the spoil has been made into banks and terraces, which act like giant storage heaters - giving back the warmth of the sun to the plants after dark. In these areas, a wider range of southern-hemisphere plants is thriving, including proteas, leucospermums and lampranthus.

Every available space on the island of Herm is gardened, including around Le Manoir.

For those visitors not heading for the beach, a woodland walk offers a route inland towards the higher points on the island. Here they will find Le Manoir, where the resident staff live in the old fortified castle keep and tower - all renovated for twenty-first-century living. Herm is a popular wedding island, and the area around Le Manoir is deliberately romantic, being planted with white roses (*Rosa* 'Wedding Day') and other wedding-themed planting (such as *Exochorda* × *macrantha* 'The Bride'). In the courtyard, staff and guests staying here on holiday can help themselves to herbs from beneath the palms.

ENVIRONMENTAL BALANCE

Gardeners are by nature used to change. Chopping down trees, opening up a view, pulling out a border that is past its best, sowing meadows and adding contemporary elements are what makes a landscape viable. However, people who have been coming to Herm for fifty or more years on a regular basis do sometimes resist such changes and don't see the need to clip back shrubs or replant areas. Nevertheless, during the past decade, new areas have been created by removing the self-seeded trees - hornbeam (*Carpinus*), blackthorn (*Prunus spinosa*) and particularly sycamore (*Acer pseudoplatanus*) - not only to open up the views towards the sea but also to create a more interesting range of spaces.

To make a better environment for people and wildlife is always going to be a fine balancing act, especially when the day boats disgorge hundreds of people every couple of hours in the summer months. A lot of what Herm is all about goes on behind the scenes. Away from view (but accessible on the weekly guided garden tour) is a new orchard of cider trees and a collection of bee hives, from which Herm honey is produced. The bees will visit the plants across the island for nectar as well as enjoying the wildflower meadow in the orchard. Within five years, Herm hopes to be collecting enough apples to make the designated 20 per cent that must be grown in the appellation area to be able to produce a 'Herm' cider. Diversification is the way to make an island sustainable, and it is good to find the natural environment at the heart of things.

OPPOSITE CLOCKWISE FROM TOP LEFT: Mediterranean stone pines (*Pinus pinea*) and holm oaks (*Quercus ilex*) above the port; *Furcraea longeava* in flower; *Phormium tenax* on the beach; the White House gardens; beehives at Le Manoir; blue morning glory (*Ipomoea*) growing through white mesembryanthemums.

WILD LEEK

There are two varieties of wild leek growing on the shores of south-west Britain and its adjacent islands: the broad-leaved *Allium ampeloprasum* and Babington's leek (*A. ampeloprasum* var. *babingtonii*). The one pictured below is Babington's leek, growing on Herm, where it makes great swathes of pale mauve flowers in late spring and early summer. It is native to many Mediterranean shores and coastal regions around the Black Sea, and may have been brought to the British Isles by prehistoric settlers. Babington's leek has naturalized throughout the south-west of Britain and its islands, producing tiny bulbils above the flower heads, which is the way it multiplies. It can be bought for garden use as a bulb or as a plant. The foliage dies back in summer, to reappear in autumn. The flowers are pretty and the leaves have a garlicky flavour, which can be used in cooking. Babington's leek prefers very well-drained soil and a sunny position.

Allium ampeloprasum var. *babingtonii*

La Seigneurie Gardens

SARK

Less than an hour's boat ride from Guernsey lies Sark, which proclaims its difference and its independence proudly. It is an island of 500 people, with no airport and no cars - the only modes of transport being horse and cart, tractor or bicycle. For more than four centuries, this 500-hectare/1,235-acre island with its dramatic coastline has been a fief with a seigneur or lord running a feudal system and defending the island in the name of the Crown. The first seigneur served under Queen Elizabeth I, and the latest under Queen Elizabeth II, although Seigneur of Sark is now only a titular role.

The title has passed through several families, but perhaps best known is Sibyl Hathaway, Dame of Sark, who inherited the fief from her father in 1927 and held it until 1974. She travelled widely and, because she spoke German, she remained in charge of the civil administration of the island during the Occupation of 1940-45. Always a controversial figure, she nevertheless made sure that Sark remained in the public eye, attracting visits from royalties and film stars.

The earliest building on the site of La Seigneurie (the house where the seigneurs live) was the Priory of Saint Magloire in the sixth century. The house itself, built in 1675, became La Seigneurie when Susanne le Pelley became dame in 1739. Successive dames and seigneurs have extended and evolved the building piecemeal. Among the most recent, Michael and Diana Beaumont in particular loved the gardens and improved them significantly. On the death of Michael in 2016, their son Christopher Beaumont became Sark's 23rd seigneur.

THE WALLED GARDEN

The centrepiece of the gardens at La Seigneurie - the high, stone-walled garden and its glasshouse - were built by the

The oldest part of the walled garden is the formal rose garden, which has compartments filled with old-fashioned roses and edged with box.

Le Pelley family between 1835 and 1841. The gardens were laid out to align with and give views to the church and to offer protection from the wind. The oldest part of the gardens is the rose garden with its box hedging. Although the glasshouse has been rebuilt, it still holds the original sliding Victorian pruning ladder – a feature of many Channel Island vineries.

The soil at La Seigneurie is crumbly, free-draining and mildly acidic, enabling camellias, hydrangeas and azaleas to grow with no supplements, and blueberries to thrive in the fruit cage. Other than these obvious signs of acidity, all the other plants are those you might find in a mainland garden. The aim is for a continuous display of interest without the work involved in bedding or annuals and the result is a fresh, ever-evolving display. It wouldn't be a garden, however, without mention of weeds, and here the 'onion weed' *Allium triquetrum* is the one that tends to be difficult to remove from the borders.

The tentative openings of the gardens to the public began under Dame Sibyl, initially one day a week but gradually increasing under Seigneur Michael Beaumont to daily opening during the main tourist season. Michael, who was responsible for much of the late-twentieth and early twenty-first-century planting and structures, worried what the future would hold as he and Diana became less able to work in the gardens. Together with Charles Maitland, they initiated the foundation of a trust that would protect the gardens' long-term interests; thus, La Seigneurie Gardens Trust was granted a fifty-year lease to run the gardens from 1 January 2009.

Maitland, who had arrived on Sark to retire and intended to do nothing much more than tend his own garden, was not at all fazed by the scale of the project, but he knew it had to be self-supporting. To that end, he invested his own money in renovating the former farm buildings around the edge of the gardens for various uses – the first being an old cowshed, which is now a thriving café leased to new tenants and bringing good revenue into the gardens. This along with entrance ticket and gift shop sales have meant that the gardens are now financially viable, employing six gardeners year-round and creating a key focus for visitors to the island.

OPPOSITE: La Seigneurie is still home to the Seigneur of Sark.

ABOVE: This area of the walled garden has a more contemporary planting scheme with standard cordylines, and grasses planted among bright red *Rosa* Glad Tidings.

LEFT: The gardeners take pride in every corner of the gardens at La Seigneurie.

FOLLOWING PAGES: Now run by La Seigneurie Gardens Trust, the gardens first opened to the public in the 1950s.

ROSA MUNDI

The apothecary's rose (*Rosa gallica* var. *officinalis*) has been grown in Europe since at least the medieval period and probably longer. Its deep pink colour was famed in the garden, but also for its myriad medicinal uses. Around 1500, a naturally occurring sport with striped pink and white petals was spotted: *Rosa gallica* 'Versicolor'. It soon became known as rosa mundi (rose of the world), after 'The Fair Rosamund' – Rosamund Clifford, the lover of Henry II and rival of Eleanor of Aquitaine. This twelfth-century story of rivalry was embroidered many times from the sixteenth century onwards, including the part where Eleanor confronts Rosamund within a labyrinth in the garden of Woodstock Park in Oxfordshire. The rose has stayed popular and is still widely grown as low hedging, being reliable, compact and with a story to tell. Its flowers are semi-double, very scented and prolific in midsummer.

Rosa gallica 'Versicolor'

THE LAYOUT

The structure owes much to previous seigneurs and particularly to Michael – an aeronautical engineer by profession, but one who learnt to garden. Nearest the house, the walled garden creates an enclosed area for roses, particularly *Rosa banksiae* 'Lutea' and *R.* 'Climbing Lady Hillingdon', and other climbing plants such as old-fashioned clematis. Outside the walled garden, the Beaumonts planted yew (*Taxus*) hedges either side of a central axis; this is now known as the daisy border as its low stone walls are covered in *Erigeron karvinskianus*. Michael built shady wooden pavilions from the timber of holm oaks (*Quercus ilex*) that had come down in the storm of 1987. One of his last projects was to install a head-height hedge maze of *Olearia paniculata;* children who make it to the centre are rewarded with the discovery of a miniature castle.

MINIMAL CHANGES

For La Seigneurie Gardens Trust this was not a case of a restoration – the gardens had been tended and were in good order. However, the trust, with six gardening staff led by Jo Birch, have tried to move to a more relaxed style of planting than the one they inherited, while keeping the structure intact. Each of the six gardeners has a particular area of responsibility: the lawns, the roses, the walled garden, the vegetable garden and so on. The kitchen garden was and still is used to supply vegetables, espaliered fruit and salads for the occupants and staff of the house, with any surplus going to Hathaway's Café or being sold off to visitors. Locals still arrive bearing cloth bags to take home windfall apples and buy sweetcorn for their supper.

Metal arches have been put in to replace wooden ones as they aged and to make for a more interesting journey through the space. Pathways have been put through overlarge beds, to bring visitors closer to the plants, and there is an emphasis on scent, long flowering and texture, rather than just colour. Michael's holm oak pavilions are still solid, but have been used as shady fern arbours – the sound of water from pebble pools made them inviting places to rest on a hot day.

OPPOSITE CLOCKWISE FROM TOP LEFT: *Rosa* 'Rambling Rector', *Rosa* 'Tuscany Superb', *Centaurea cyanus*, *Nigella damascena* and scented dianthus beneath mophead hydrangeas, *Nepeta* 'Six Hills Giant' with *Rosa* Super Fairy, *Rosa* Tess of the d'Urbervilles, *Hordeum jubatum*, *Lathyrus odoratus*, *Rosa* The Pilgrim.

Within the walled garden, the old rose garden is still in its original position - replanted with *Rosa* 'Tuscany Superb' and rosa mundi (*R. gallica* 'Versicolor'; see box, page 118). For the Millennium, the Beaumonts laid out a second, circular rose garden, which the trust has now replanted with English shrub roses and climbers - the roses encircle a central sundial edged with *Nepeta* 'Six Hills Giant'.

Throughout the gardens are many clues as to La Seigneurie's colourful history. A short path emerges at the monastic fish ponds and woodland. Much of the woodland on Sark was cleared during the Second World War for timber and to enable clear signalling to Guernsey, which is 11-13 kilometres/7-8 miles away across the water; the woodland is now recolonizing, mainly with sycamore (*Acer pseudoplatanus*) and oaks (*Quercus*). An old apple crusher in the courtyard is a reminder of the Channel Islands' rich heritage of cider production, while on the battery a bronze canon, given to the first seigneur by Elizabeth I in 1572, still faces out to sea. The Victorian colombier, or dovecote, was a feature of many Channel Island manor houses.

A SECURE FUTURE

The beginnings of La Seigneurie Gardens Trust in 2008 coincided with the first democratic elections on Sark. The island is no longer feudal, but there is still a seigneur at La Seigneurie and most people feel that is as it should be - albeit a seigneur who no longer has responsibility for the gardens. Within the trust's parameters, the gardeners are given quite a lot of freedom in their work, dreaming up new planting schemes each year and making subtle changes which are enhancing these special gardens.

OPPOSITE ABOVE: The arches of the nineteenth-century walled garden were deliberately built to align with Sark's church.
OPPOSITE BELOW: Any surplus from the working vegetable garden is sold to locals and visitors to help support the gardens at La Seigneurie.
ABOVE: A sundial surrounded by *Nepeta* 'Six Hills Giant' marks the centre of the romantic Millennium Rose Garden, where modern roses are underplanted with *Erigeron karvinskianus*.

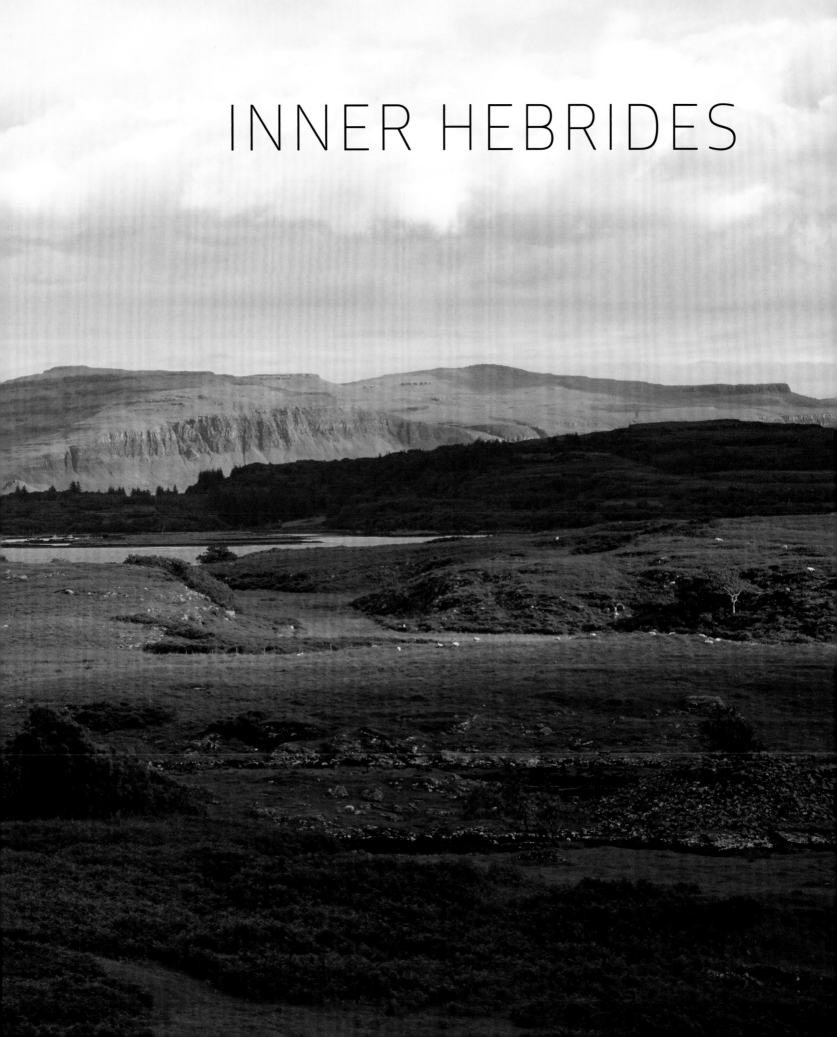

INNER HEBRIDES

THE INNER HEBRIDES is a string of islands also known as the Inner Isles (Na h-Eileanan a-staigh) to distinguish them from the Outer Hebrides (Na h-Eileanan Siar; Western Isles), which lie to the north-west. The Inner Isles are made up of thirty-five inhabited islands, including some that have achieved almost mythical status (through song and whisky), such as Skye, Mull and Islay. Each of these islands is unique in its climate, soil, underlying rocks, cultural history and traditions, although it's probably true to say that no one ever went to the Hebrides purely for the gardens - the wildlife and the scenery, perhaps, but not just the gardens.

What draws these islands together is the proximity of the sea - not just its climatic influence, which makes the summers cool, the winters mild and the climate wet, but also the fact that, historically, it was the seas around the islands that were the main thoroughfares and first line of defence. Island history is also the history of clans: the MacLeods of Skye, for example, and the Macleans of Mull. Being built for defence, their castles don't always have gardens. However, on Skye there is an interesting garden surrounding the ruins of Armadale Castle, which is lovely in spring, and also at Dunvegan Castle, which has a lush water garden behind its forbidding exterior.

The castles may have taken most of the best sites, but there are many more modest homesteads that typify the difficulties and rewards of gardening on this terrain.

PREVIOUS PAGES: The north-western coast of Mull presents a rugged landscape - quite a challenge for any gardener.
OPPOSITE: Originally designed in the eighteenth century, the gardens at Dunvegan Castle on Skye have been replanted by successive generations of the Clan MacLeod.
ABOVE RIGHT: Dating back to the twelfth century, Dunvegan Castle commands the sea to Skye via Loch Dunvegan.
RIGHT: The ruined castle at Armadale on Skye is the focus of formal and woodland gardens, part of the Clan Donald estate.

Lip Na Cloiche
MULL

'Of isles, the fairest . . . the first and rarest' is the way Dugald MacPhail poetically described Mull in his song *An t-Eilean Muileach*. If this makes Mull sound like a soft, gentle place, then the reality is far more challenging. Particularly in the north of the island, it has a largely volcanic landscape, shaped by ice to form corries, inland lochs and scree slopes. Despite thousands of years of soil accumulation, cultivating the land has never been easy.

Gardens rarely live up to the name given to the house, but in the case of Lip na Cloiche the name is an exact fit: the translation from Gaelic being 'Edge of the Rock'. The house occupies the only flat ground on this 0.4 hectare/1 acre of steeply sloping rock on the north-western coast of the island, overlooking Loch Tuath and the Isle of Ulva. The prevailing winds come from the south-west, bringing in salt-laden gales and a high level of moisture, meaning that only the very determined gardener will succeed.

OPPOSITE: The vegetable garden at Lip na Cloiche takes the full force of the south-westerly winds.
BELOW: The traditional-style house is surrounded with interesting and unusual plants.

Such a person is Lucy Mackenzie Panizzon, who decided immediately that she would accept any damage the weather might bring rather than sacrifice any view. In 2000, after years of living in Italy, she chose an old bothy looking out over the outer islands as her future home. She rebuilt it as a traditional-style cottage and moved back to Mull, the island where she was born and which had been her home as a child.

People need a certain type of mentality to thrive on an island where only a self-sufficient, multi-tasking approach makes life possible. Single-handedly, Mackenzie removed the gorse and bracken that covered the slope and took in an extra strip of land to give access to the burn that tumbles down one side of the plot. She then painstakingly laid out a series of paths and terraces to give access to the full height of the plot, building walls with the stones reclaimed from the old bothy and making paths with materials gleaned from the beach.

There was little soil and much of it had to barrowed in from molehills in neighbouring fields. Anything found in the hills, hedgerows or shoreline was put to use, such as edging the borders with driftwood and old iron from bedsteads and farm machinery. Salvaged fishing rope and nets were used as plant supports and railings.

PLANTING PARADISE

Lip na Cloiche would be a remarkable collection of plants if it were on mainland Britain, but when set against the bracken-covered rock faces that lie to either side it is a staggering achievement. There was no masterplan, but Mackenzie wanted to avoid rhododendrons so began to experiment with a wider range of herbaceous plants and shrubs. Guided by her own interests and knowledge of what might grow there, she was soon propagating plants and setting up a nursery selling plants that do well in these conditions. Despite the salt-laden winds, this stretch of Mull is one of the mildest areas of the island, protected by the smaller islands of Ulva and Gometra, with the Treshnish Isles and Staffa beyond. Snow is occasional in winter and usually disappears quickly, allowing a surprising number of plants to stay in the ground unscathed.

The south-west-facing garden at Lip na Cloiche has been carved out of a barren, gorse-covered hillside.

Mull is generally a well-wooded island – if there were no deer or sheep, ash, birch, rowan and oak would seed and grow into mature trees. But on this plot only one ash had thrived. This meant that hedging was crucial to the garden's success – *Escallonia macrantha* to the east, *Griselinia littoralis* 'Variegata' on the western boundary and a low hedge of *Fuchsia magellanica* on the south-western front, so as not to block the view. The hedges can sometimes be blackened by a late frost, especially when the new growth has already started, but in general all three plants do the job they are intended for.

The burn at Lip na Cloiche offered the most immediate opportunities for planting. However, the soil around it was not at all moist and only around the ash tree is it deep enough to support candelabra primulas in spring. Mackenzie cleverly chose plants with a 'water garden look' but which are quite happy in ordinary soil: *Darmera peltata*, *Ligularia* 'Britt Marie Crawford', *Rodgersia pinnata* 'Perthshire Bronze', *Rheum palmatum* 'Red Herald', *Inula magnifica*, *Aralia racemosa* and *Astilboides tabularis*. She also chose woodland plants that enjoy the shaded position: *Diphylleia cymosa,* disporums, meconopsis and the airy *Thalictrum* 'Elin'.

Island gardens do not necessarily behave like 'seaside' gardens. Many of the typical seaside shrubs that *should* take the winds, such as tamarix, struggle at Lip na Cloiche. Yet other wind-hardy shrubs such as *Olearia traversii*, *O. arborescens* and *O. chathamica*, *Pittosporum tenuifolium* 'Irene Paterson', *Tasmannia lanceolata*, *Ceanothus cyaneus* and willows such as *Salix magnifica* and *S. fargesii* do well here. Two buddlejas have also made the grade: *Buddleja loricata*, with its narrow leaves and clusters of creamy white flowers, and the purple-flowered *B. salviifolia*.

THE LIP NA CLOICHE YEAR

The year has a natural rhythm for Mackenzie, as it does for many islanders. In summer, she is to be found either in the garden, talking about plants with visitors, or in the house looking after bed-and-breakfast guests. By mid-autumn, she will begin the seasonal tidy-up, cutting back the perennials and plant stems. On Mull, it would be folly to leave standing material in winter to enjoy the skeletal forms – here, they are soon turned to black mush, or are knocked over by the wind.

In winter Mackenzie's 'real' work starts: combing the shoreline, fields and moors for anything that can be used in either her artwork or in the garden, as well as doing the essential tasks of rebuilding walls or relaying paths and steps. She also collects seaweed from the beach to put on to the vegetable garden and any newly made borders. Existing borders will get an application of home-made compost if there is enough to go round. Nothing is imported from garden centres, so if it can't be found the plants must do without.

LEVELS OF INTEREST

Looking at the deeds in 2007, Mackenzie discovered that the boundary fence had been put in the wrong position and she actually owned another 10m/33ft of near-vertical hillside. The bank fence was therefore moved to its present position, allowing more room for planting. The hill acts as a run-off system for water, making the garden as a whole well-drained,

OPPOSITE: The eastern side of the plot is surrounded by hedges of *Escallonia macrantha*.
ABOVE LEFT: The banks of the natural burn have been planted with ferns, *Darmera peltata* and rodgersiaso.
ABOVE RIGHT: Plantswoman Lucy Mackenzie has utilized every bit of the steeply sloping plot.

although the top terrace is particularly dry - as well as windy.

This is a garden that works for all ages and levels of horticultural interest: children are excited by the winding paths and the unconventional use of materials; non-gardeners are drawn to the quirky collections of found objects; and there is also more than enough to intrigue the most learned plantsperson. Mackenzie worked in other nurseries and gardens before setting up her own, and her plant tastes are a mixture of personal choice and hard-won experience.

She favours unusual evergreen shrubs such as *Daphniphyllum macropodum* and *Ozothamnus rosmarinifolius* 'Silver Jubilee',

ABOVE: In the front garden are thriving plantings of mauve *Campanula lactiflora* 'Prichard's Variety' and pale yellow *Thalictrum flavum*.
OPPOSITE: The side garden at Lip Na Cloiche is packed with cottage-garden plants, including red valerian, salvias and veronicastrums.

a little-used plant that has proved to be virtually deer-proof. Hebes are also considered invaluable, but the variety needs to be carefully chosen - approximately half of the standard ones don't tolerate the wind (the purple-leaved varieties being particularly prone to cold). On the other hand, *Hebe salicifolia* is almost a weed and, given the chance, will seed everywhere and need to be removed. *Hydrangea aspera* is treasured, as are any roses that survive: *Rosa glauca*, *R. moyesii*, *R.* 'New Dawn' and the big scrambling *R.* 'Paul's Himalayan Musk' grow along the top boundary. Mackenzie is also fond of clematis; while the small-flowered montanas and tanguticas do well, the large-flowered, mid-season clematis will not thrive without help - they are one of the few exceptions to the 'no-pampering' rule and get a regular dose of tomato food.

In terms of perennials, hardy geraniums are given as much space as possible, *G.* 'Orion' and *G. clarkei* 'Kashmir

ABOVE LEFT: Every path was hand laid, using found materials.

ABOVE RIGHT: Old fishing ropes create height and somewhere useful on which to train climbing hops.

RIGHT: Driftwood from the beach has become a seat for visitors.

OPPOSITE: Winters at Lip na Cloiche are spent combing for objects discarded in the fields or washed up on the beach – from fishing tackle and chains to disused shovels. They all contribute to the unique character of the garden.

Purple' grow on the terraces, while *G. palmatum* is allowed to spread outside the greenhouse and elsewhere. The stonecrop *Hylotelephium telephium* 'Red Cauli' adds late colour and is reliable. Monkshoods (*Aconitum napellus*) have proved to be easier than delphiniums, while bush echium (*Echium candicans*) is only borderline hardy. As in other west-coast gardens, tree echium (*E. pininana*) does well, but takes longer to flower, being triennial or even quadrennial.

SELF-SUFFICIENCY

If Mull were a desert island, then Mackenzie's 'luxury' item would be the greenhouse. Kept to a minimum of 4°C/39°F and used for propagation and growing tomatoes in summer, the greenhouse along with the small vegetable plot allows her to be self-sufficient in vegetables - another essential, when the nearest store is a long drive along a single-track road.

Anything that is slightly tender, such as salvias, are grown from cuttings each year, including Mackenzie's particular favourite - the dark purple, almost black *Salvia* 'Amistad'. The large numbers of pots of pelargoniums and nemesia are moved to the greenhouse in winter and cuttings taken, to make sure there is enough stock for next year.

In the vegetable garden, French beans are trained over tepees of driftwood. As the garden faces south-west, all the typical kitchen garden crops can be grown here, including broad beans, shallots, ruby chard, peas, brassicas, cavolo nero, leeks and even sweetcorn; they are started off in the greenhouse and put outdoors when they reach 45cm/18in tall. Courgettes are raised on the compost heap, with old roofing slates used to absorb the heat of the sun.

Sometimes in a garden it is the small things that mark it out as something special. Walking round, visitors might not look down at their feet to notice the ground cover that has been carefully chosen: *Pachysandra terminalis*, *Acaena saccaticupula* 'Blue Haze' and the woody, low-growing willow *Salix nakamurana* var. *yezoalpin*a with its soft, rounded leaves. But they certainly will notice the individual plant labels in the nursery sales benches, beautifully handwritten on razor clam shells, collected from the beach after an autumn storm.

LEFT FROM TOP: *Ozothamnus rosmarinifolius* 'Silver Jubilee', *Hebe* 'White Wand', *Geranium psilostemon*.

ABOVE: The greenhouse is a necessary adjunct to the garden, as it is used to raise plants for the nursery.

LEFT: Small raised beds made from driftwood enable the owner to be self-sufficent in herbs, salads and most vegetables.

Priory Garden
ORONSAY

Oronsay – a tiny tidal island off Colonsay – must be one of the most remote inhabited islands of the Hebrides. In a straight line to the west, nothing but a lighthouse stands between it and North America. There are no near neighbours, although Mull, Islay and Jura can all be seen from different vantage points. The coast of Donegal is just visible to the south, and the story goes that St Columba set foot on Oronsay but decided not to found a monastery there as he did not want his new community to grieve for their homeland of Ireland. He moved on to Iona and, although there is no historical basis for the story, there are many links between the priories of Iona and Oronsay.

Geologically, Colonsay and Oronsay belong, along with Instrahull off the tip of Ireland, to a distinct 'Colonsay Group' separated by a fault line from all their neighbours. Some 1,800 million years ago, they were connected to Greenland and have travelled 1,300 kilometres/800 miles to the south, marking them out as even more distinctive. When translated from the Norse, Oronsay means Ebb-Tide Island. It can be reached only by walking across The Strand from Colonsay, in short windows of opportunity when the tide is low.

The 600 hectares/1,500 acres of Oronsay Farm, which is in effect the whole island, were sold in 1984 to the Colburns from Massachusetts, who fell in love with the house and walled garden, in spite of the inconvenience of being totally cut off by the tide for all but a few hours every day. The property stands next to Oronsay Priory (a Scottish scheduled monument).

I.W. Colburn (Ike) and his wife Frannie were both excited by the idea of transforming this remote farm into their island home. As an architect, Ike had been responsible for many of the US's mid-twentieth-century domestic and ecclesiastical buildings and had been on the boards of the Chicago Botanic Garden, the Pacific Botanic Garden (now known as National Tropical

The Priory Garden at Oronsay Farm was designed by Penelope Hobhouse in the late 1980s.

Botanic Garden) on Kauai, Hawaii and the Massachusetts Horticultural Society. After they had bought Oronsay and Ike had remodelled the cottages and steadings, they decided to make something of the old walled priory gardens.

THE DESIGNER'S MARK

This walled enclosure had seen previous use as a sheepfold and, since their arrival, as a vegetable garden run as a business by their neighbour, as the Colburns were not there year-round. In 1988, they decided to call in the renowned garden designer Penelope Hobhouse to design something completely new and rather bold.

She set about designing a series of rooms, which not only were fashionable in the late 1980s and early 1990s but were also ideally suited to the windswept conditions of Oronsay. The climate there is typical of the Western Isles of Scotland, with average temperatures rarely below freezing in winter but with severe gales. Summers are cool but sunny, and rainfall moderately high. Hedging would be key to the planting scheme. After toying with the idea of escallonia, they settled on privet (*Ligustrum*), which, although not typical in the Hebrides, does have the bonus of fast re-leafing after it has been scorched by the wind.

Initially, each compartment had a theme (reflecting the way a monastery layout is ordered and named - refectory, dormitory and so on). This translated into functional enclosures: spring garden, vegetable garden, shrub garden and autumn garden, as well as the 'Jekyll-Thaxter Garden' to reflect the work of two great plantswomen from either side of the Atlantic - Gertrude Jekyll (1843-1932), from Surrey, England, and Celia Thaxter 1835-1894, author of *An Island Garden*, who gardened on the Isles of Shoals off the coast of Maine and New Hampshire, USA.

For the first year, Hobhouse advised growing nothing but potatoes in order to clear the ground of weeds before planting began. Following that, she specified plants that would suit the concept of each enclosure: *Rosa gallica* var. *officinalis*, rosemary and teucrium in the 'Medieval' enclosure, for example. Although the plants themselves have been replaced, Hobhouse's basic plan remains.

Within the privet hedging, she designed an enclosure for shrubs that would deal with the conditions. These included hebes, olearia and *Griselinia littoralis*. There was a garden for autumn flowers, filled with asters, and another specifically for early summer with phlomis and other plants that could thrive within the protection of the hedges such as geraniums and sisyrinchiums.

The soil in the Oronsay Priory enclosed garden is mainly shell sand, so slightly alkaline in contrast to the naturally acid moorland soil just over the wall. It is also well drained and had been richly improved over time with manure from the Oronsay farm's cattle. This has enabled a good range of plants to have been grown, including grapes, apples, medlars, strawberries and even figs in a good year. To create more shelter, willow hurdles were erected within the framework of hedging, and this allowed roses and a range of herbaceous plants to be grown. Outside the walls, a shelter belt of rowan (*Sorbus aucuparia*) added yet another barrier.

NATURAL EVOLUTION

The garden has inevitably changed over the three decades since Hobhouse's original design was set out. The original willow hurdles succumbed to old age and have been replaced with 1.5m/5ft panels of sturdy local timber, horizontally slatted to allow the wind to flow through them, rather than up and over them, thereby limiting any damage.

Many of the choice plants specified by Hobhouse have been replanted with ones that are more widely available to the gardeners on Oronsay. However, *Rosa rugosa* (a sturdy shrub rose that grows wild on the shores of Massachusetts and equally well in Scotland), *Olearia traversii* and *Hebe pinguifolia* 'Pagei' continue to thrive. Hobhouse herself is sanguine about the changes, remarking that gardens are always designed for the here and now - and should never be thought of as 'forever'.

Ike Colburn died in 1992, just two years after the garden was laid out, but the family continue to treasure his and Hobhouse's combined vision, while encouraging a more bio-diverse approach to the land as a whole.

OPPOSITE CLOCKWISE FROM TOP LEFT: The formal layout of the Oronsay Priory garden; roses thrive on the shell sand; *Rosa rugosa*; Oronsay sheep; privet hedging, which is used to make the 'rooms'; Oronsay Priory was dedicated to St Columba; horizontal slatted timber screens deflect the wind; Oronsay's resident peacocks.

There are two pairs of nesting corncrakes on Oronsay and leaving the meadows uncut until late in the year provides cover for this declining species.

The land on Oronsay is now farmed by the Royal Society for the Protection of Birds (RSPB) largely for birds – and in particular choughs and corncrakes. The chough (a member of the crow family with bright red legs and bills) has only sixty breeding pairs across the whole of Scotland, and by following careful farming practices Oronsay has also been able to support a couple of nesting pairs. The mixed farming regime of cattle and sheep, arable and late-cut fields for corncrake conservation (a declining species that can be clearly heard but rarely seen among the long, rough grass) complements the other areas, which are grazed short to give visiting choughs access to insects. The farm's cattle produce plentiful manure, which encourages invertebrates and is used in the walled garden. The whole island is a Site of Special Scientific Interest (SSSI).

This kind of farming, known as 'high nature value farming', has had a much wider impact on the island flora, which is home to sheets of wildflower grassland (machair), wild roses, wild thyme, honeysuckle and abundant orchids (see opposite).

Colonsay itself has a varied landscape of dunes and tidal plains, acid grassland and a very interesting woodland garden at Colonsay House, at its best in spring when the rhododendrons are at their peak. Low-lying these islands may be, but they more than make up for it in botanical interest.

WILD FLOWERS

The linked islands of Colonsay and Oronsay have become a great place to see orchids and other wild flowers growing within the machair. Machair is a particularly rare type of coastal habitat, existing only on north-western shores, in Ireland and on some Scottish islands. It refers to the area of land between the beach and the peat moors, which may be cultivated or grazed, but is often home to wildflower grasslands.

On Oronsay, one of the most prolific wild flowers in summer is the heath spotted orchid (*Dactylorhiza maculata*), which enjoys the heath conditions across the central part of the island. It is not rare in the British Isles, but it is most likely to be found in the west, flowering from late spring into summer. It is a close relation of the common spotted orchid (*D. fuchsii*) – also found on the islands. Bees and other insects visiting these orchids are drawn by the scent, but are not rewarded with any nectar.

Other orchids to be seen there in early summer include lesser butterfly orchid (*Platanthera bifolia*), which is scented and marked to attract moths at night and pollinating insects by day. It is another heath and grassland orchid that is endangered in the south of Britain, where its habitat is less widespread; it is more plentiful in the north-west.

The late-flowering lady's tresses orchid *Spiranthes romanzoffiana* was first found growing at Uragaig on Colonsay in 1930. Once exceedingly rare, it is now increasing because of the short sward regime, which benefits the choughs.

Other wild flowers that proliferate on both islands are heaths and heathers such as bell heather (*Erica cinerea*) as well as wild thyme (*Thymus polytrichus* subsp. *britannicus*).

To see the machair in full flower, visit the islands between May and June, when 1 sq. m/1 sq. yard of grassland can house up to forty-five different wildflower species.

Platanthera bifolia

Dactylorhiza maculata

Thymus polytrichus subsp. *britannicus*

Erica cinerea

An Cala

SEIL

The Isle of Seil (Gaelic: Saoil) might just be the one Scottish island you have never heard of. Separated from the mainland by the narrowest of crossings, it requires close scrutiny of the maps to see that it really is an island at all. Historically, its fame was due to the fine-quality slate that was quarried there and, more intensively, on the island of Easdale; together, they became known as the Slate Islands. Easdale slate was shipped widely, roofing most of the tenement buildings in Glasgow; at its peak, five million slates were exported around the world every year. Quarrying was brought to an end by a tidal wave that flooded the quarries in 1891, and the last slates finally left the Slate Islands in 1911.

The history of Seil may be more industrial than romantic, but the islanders cherish that heritage and their Atlantic Bridge – built in 1792 to cross what feels no more than a river. It is nevertheless, they claim, the only genuine bridge across the Atlantic Ocean.

OPPOSITE: A flock of Rupert Till's wirework sheep are positioned on the upper lawn of An Cala.
BELOW: The house was originally three workers' cottages and a whisky distillery; it was made into one unit in the 1930s.

A GAELIC HAVEN

An Cala (meaning 'harbour' or 'haven') lies on the south-west of Seil, near the village of Ellenabeich (island of birches) - itself an island before waste slate formed a causeway to make it just another village on Seil. The house is formed from three former workers' cottages along with a building used as an unofficial whisky distillery - a common practice before the 1823 Excise Act put whisky production on to a more regular footing.

The 2-hectare/5-acre plot that comprises An Cala was bought in 1930 by Colonel Murray, later Lord Elibank. Each cottage was on a different level, but he managed to convert them into one house for himself and his new wife, actress Faith Celli - feted on the London stage for her portrayal of Peter Pan in the play by J.M. Barrie. Wanting to make the most of the sloping ground, with its natural waterfall and sea views, Murray engaged the Cumbrian landscape architect Thomas Mawson to draw up plans for a garden made from local materials.

Making use of the shelter belt of sitka spruce (*Picea sitchensis*) already planted by Murray, Mawson created what was essentially an Arts & Crafts garden - informed by the idea that a garden should never be seen all at once but should constitute a 'journey'. Mawson's men took a full year to carry out the construction, lodging in Ellenabeich while they worked. Dynamite, which was in good supply in a quarrying community, was used to break up the natural rock and create the driveway, while slate was brought in to build the terraces, steps and rockery.

Mawson left the bedrock *in situ*, in various places, to give this garden a satisfying balance of designed and natural landscaping. Where the bedrock is barely covered, the natural moorland plants such as saxifrage and heaths have colonized the acid soil, while in the deeper pockets of imported soil (brought in as ballast on the slate ships and carried up to An Cala by horse and cart) most plants will thrive - from clematis to tree peonies.

Gardening on this site, which faces Labrador and gets the full force of the Atlantic winds, would not have been possible had not Murray installed a 4.5m/15ft-high grey brick wall. Bricks are not part of vernacular architecture in Argyll, and they had to be sourced from a works in southern England - at least they matched the colouring of the local stone. Unfortunately

Designed by Thomas Mawson in the 1930s, An Cala's garden looks out to Ellenabeich and the island of Easdale.

ABOVE LEFT: A natural stream flows down the rock into the garden at An Cala.

ABOVE RIGHT: Mawson directed the stream's flow into a series of rills and stepped watercourses.

RIGHT: Beside a bridge, the stream bank is planted with yellow *Lysimachia punctata* and pink filipendula.

OPPOSITE: Where the rock outcropped naturally - as by the pool - Mawson left it *in situ*.

for Murray, the stock of bricks was finite and there was only enough to enclose part of the garden, leaving the western half of the plot much more exposed.

Concerned about the future of the garden, Colonel Murray sold An Cala to his friends Captain and Mrs Blakeney who cared for it until the late 1980s. In 1987, a Historic Environment Scotland survey designated the garden as an outstanding Work of Art, and this was the same year that Sheila Downie and her husband Tom decided to buy An Cala. Having both originated from Glasgow, they had been looking for a Scottish home to return to after working out in Saudi Arabia. They bought An Cala sight unseen, but Sheila had already fallen for the garden. On arrival, she began the gentle restoration of the Mawson garden.

An Cala is a garden of rooms, although very different to those formal compartments built in the south of England on level terrain. Rather, it is a meandering series of encounters that still delights eighty years later. Nothing from the original layout has been changed except, inevitably, the plants themselves. Japanese cherry (*Prunus serrulata*) trees, which were fashionable in Britain during the early twentieth century, were showing their age when the Downies arrived and needed propping up. Meanwhile, new ones were planted along the drive. A few of the original Japanese maples (*Acer palmatum*), small-leaved azaleas and an interesting grafted standard *Cotoneaster horizontalis* survived, but the herbaceous and water planting reflects Sheila's taste rather than the Murrays'.

The burn at An Cala tumbles over the rock behind the garden as an impressive waterfall and Mawson enhanced this by manipulating the water as it made its way down towards the shore. Pipes were put in underground to take the full flow, while the surface water was dammed to make a series of ponds. This has facilitated some of the most vibrant planting in

the garden with yellow *Lysimachia punctata*, pink filipendulas, thalictrums, yellow mimulus, astrantias, astilbes, *Darmera peltata*, polygonatums and dicentras lining the watercourse.

Over the years, Sheila has planted shrubs she likes and that do well - abutilons against the house and hydrangeas in the borders, particularly *Hydrangea aspera* Villosa Group, *H. arborescens* 'Annabelle' and white *H. macrophylla* 'Madame Emile Mouillère'. The parallel rectangular borders outside the conservatory were originally rose beds, planted with the bright pink *Rosa* 'Betty Prior', the height of fashion in the 1930s. These have now been replaced with traditional herbaceous planting, although *R.* 'Betty Prior' lives on, edging the upper terraces. Sheila loves roses, but admits defeat with most of the old-fashioned ones, which suffer with the damp and heavy rains. Two that do well here are *R.* 'New Dawn' and *R.* Bonica and also the Pemberton roses, such as *R.* 'Penelope'.

A rectangular pool with covered summer house was a social necessity in the 1930s, and despite the less than good weather was well used by the Murrays and their friends. Sheila has made her own mark on this area, lining the walls of the summer house with collected cones and natural materials. It was a task that took two years in the run-up to the Millennium and was inspired by a similar Bavarian summer house at Brodick Castle on the Isle of Arran (see page 36).

Gardens are not all about history - they are about people - and thirty years on from taking over An Cala the Downies are still passionate about the garden and sharing it with visitors. It is sometimes hard to believe that this tranquil, waterside garden emerged from a grimy industrial past, forged by flood and dynamite.

OPPOSITE: The upper formal pool was used for bathing during the 1930s.

ABOVE: The steps leading up to the pool are typical of Mawson's landscaping, as they are of local slate and granite.

LEFT: The intricate interior design of the pavilion was handmade by Sheila Downie, using collected pine cones.

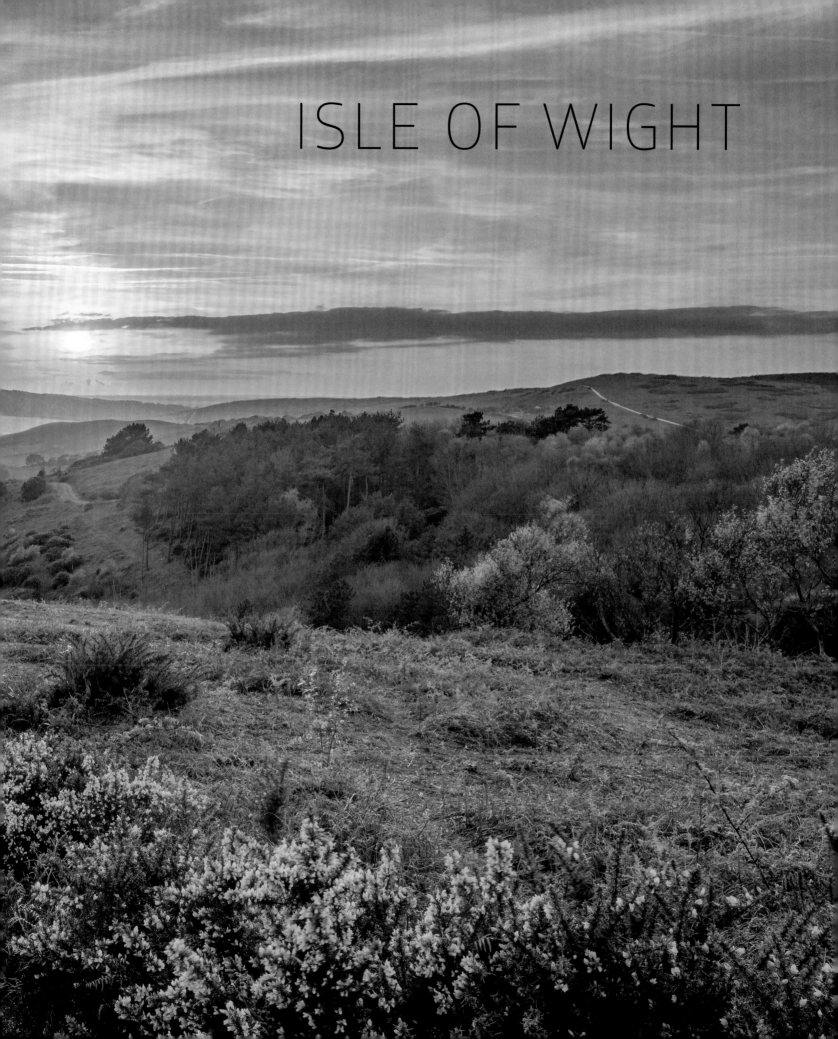

ISLE OF WIGHT

ONCE A SEPARATE KINGDOM run by Jutish kings, Wihtwara became a Norman lordship and was finally subsumed into England in the seventh century. Its independence is now long forgotten, although locals always refer to the Isle of Wight as 'the island' and occasionally to the mainland as 'North Island'.

At approximately 400 square kilometres/155 square miles, the Isle of Wight is one of the larger and more populated islands off Britain. Its two thousand hours of sunshine a year, lack of frosts and soft underlying clays, chalks and sands have meant that there is a long tradition of horticulture. Market gardening is still one of the key activities, particularly salad crops in the Arreton valley and more recently garlic growing and vineyards.

Since Queen Victoria and Prince Albert bought and rebuilt Osborne near Cowes in the mid-nineteenth century, the Isle of Wight has become a popular holiday destination. For many, it is the landforms themselves that are the attraction - the sweeping downs and the geological anomaly of the chalk inclines that dip towards the west, culminating in the Needles and the cliffs around Freshwater Bay. For other visitors it is the public and private gardens. Also, the western side is considerably less built up and includes land owned by the National Trust and large areas that together have been designated as an Area of Outstanding Natural Beauty (AONB).

PREVIOUS PAGES: The restored heathland of Mottistone Common is an area of gorse and heather - and is home to the rare Dartford warbler.
LEFT: The shallow waters of Newtown Creek are an important saltmarsh habitat.

Mottistone
Gardens

Stretching from Mottistone Down to the shore of Compton Bay, the manor of Mottistone has been known in written records since the Domesday Book and archaeologically since at least the Bronze Age. At the centre of this 263-hectare/650-acre estate is a Tudor house, which encloses a Saxon hall. The name Mottistone means 'moot stone', a standing stone, which is still visible above the long barrow behind the house, and was used by the Saxons as a meeting place.

Despite the age of the house, Mottistone does not have a particularly historic garden. It was a working farm, and the area around the house was used for penning cattle and stabling horses. In 1703, a great storm washed the bank to the east up against the house, almost burying it. From that point its fortunes declined until the 1920s, when General Jack Seely became the 1st Lord Mottistone and chose to live in this somewhat run-down building. Seely's military career is perhaps less well known than that of his horse Warrior, which, after surviving horrific front-line duty in the First World War, earned his retirement running in the surf on Compton Bay sands. Warrior was painted by Sir Alfred Munnings and had an adoring public, encouraging Seely to publish regular updates about the horse's health in *The Times*. Warrior was posthumously awarded a medal for bravery.

A FLEDGLING GARDEN

The garden to the north of the house was initially laid out with a double herbaceous border and productive garden all enclosed by privet (*Ligustrum*) hedging. Its story begins to get more interesting in 1926, when Jack Seely's son John, a young architect in London, took on the restoration of the manor house at Mottistone with his partner Paul Paget. Jack knew Edwin Lutyens and, not quite trusting his son's youthful enthusiasm, asked Lutyens to take a look at the plans.

To the north of the old manor house, steps flanked by agapanthus and *Erigeron karvinskianus* lead up to the double herbaceous border.

Lutyens is reputed to have responded by saying that the boys had done a good job keeping the house 'modest in manner' – a play on Mottistone Manor. In summer 1938, Seely & Paget (as their firm was called; it went on to design the Courtauld house at Eltham Palace) moved their working 'shack' to the garden at Mottistone, where they spent every summer until the end of their careers. They had plans for landscaping the 2.5 hectares/6 acres of gardens, but they were never realized. Jack Seely died in 1947 and for the next sixteen years the gardens were not a focus of attention.

A SIXTIES REVIVAL

The garden's change in fortunes came with the arrival of Sir John Nicholson, Jack Seely's stepson from his second marriage, soon after 1963. Although not inheriting the estate (which was bequeathed to the National Trust in 1963), Sir John took up the tenancy of Mottistone with his wife Lady Vivien and the Nicholsons were responsible for reviving the garden.

Lady Vivien, who had been brought up in Sicily, threw her heart and soul into the task. She lowered walls and instructed terraces to be made with the stones, and also designed steps to sweep down to the house. She replanted the double herbaceous border and put in boundaries of hornbeam (*Carpinus*) and yew (*Taxus*). Back home in Sicily, their gardener had always said to her: 'let's go and cause a riot in the garden!' and this became her mantra.

Lady Vivien's enthusiasm for plants transformed this sleepy place into a vibrant garden. Her style was eclectic – her borders mixed perennials such as catmint (*Nepeta*) with annual snapdragons (*Antirrhinum*), asters, zinnias, petunias and cosmos. She planted roses and put in upright junipers (*Juniperus*) to remind her of Sicily. She disliked the 'wasp-ridden' apple orchard, so grubbed it out and replaced it with an avenue of spring-flowering trees: crab apples (*Malus*), cherries (*Prunus avium*, *P. cerasus*) and almonds (*P. dulcis*). From her bedroom window, Vivien could look down over a garden that was a marriage of English and continental influences.

The gardens extend north and south of the house while the entire estate runs down to the seashore.

GARDEN DEVELOPMENT

When head gardener Robert Moore started work there in 1985, the Nicholsons were still very active in the garden and that continuity of input has been of great value. However, this is not a historic garden in National Trust terms, and therefore change has also been possible. After a full garden survey of 2004, it was suggested that Mottistone could provide a testing ground to indicate what plants might grow well in a future of climate change. As a result of this new environmental approach, Lady Vivien's taste for bedding plants could no longer be maintained, and Mottistone Gardens is now the trust's most southerly 'dry' garden. The Isle of Wight is not self-sufficient in water, which has to be piped in from the mainland; therefore it is vital that this 'no-watering' policy is adhered to.

In an effort to reduce the areas of grass, the lawned terrace nearest the house has been replaced with a vibrant planting of dahlias, *Agapanthus africanus* (see box, page 163), African daisies (*Arctotis*) and yellow *Euryops chrysanthemoides*. The colour scheme here and in the border nearest the Tea Garden is reds, oranges and blue, although a few vivid pink penstemons have crept in - Lady Vivien would most likely have approved of such flamboyant 'breaking of the rules'.

The double herbaceous border has become a purely perennial one, planted with drought-resistant perennials that will cope with the light, sandy soil. In an attempt to move towards total organic status, the roses that used to get black spot have been substituted with hardier, more disease-resistant varieties such as *Rosa* Bonica and *R.* 'Roseraie de l'Haÿ'.

Pinks (*Dianthus*) and compact lavender such as *Lavandula angustifolia* 'Munstead' are also used to make 'soft' edges. *Teucrium chamaedrys* is another favourite since it encourages hummingbird hawk-moths; it is cut back hard each spring.

THE MONOCOT BORDERS

Between 2004 and 2006, the idea was gradually developed of making borders using monocotyledon plants (whose seedlings have one, rather than two, first leaves). A monocot border may not sound very exciting but has actually evolved

OPPOSITE: The perennial borders are an eclectic mix of bright orange day lilies (*Hemerocallis*), blue catmint (*Nepeta*) and salvias, as well as deep red persicarias.

ABOVE: Lady Vivien Nicholson's flamboyant style of planting has been implemented across the terraces.

LEFT: Close to the house, blue *Agapanthus africanus*, yellow arctotis and clumps of yellow and orange dahlias can stay out year-round because of Mottistone's free-draining soil and mild winters.

ABOVE: The monocot borders show visitors the range of plants that can cope with changing climatic conditions. It includes many familiar plants such as palms, cannas, kniphofias and agapanthus.

RIGHT: In the Lower Garden, a circular maze mown in the grass is a simple and effective way to make a boring lawn more interesting - particularly for children.

into something that is very much of the twenty-first century. Monocots include many of the plants that do well in a warmer climate, such as cannas, bamboos, pampas grass (*Cortaderia*), zebra grass (*Miscanthus sinensis* 'Zebrinus'), astelias, red hot pokers (*Kniphofia*), bananas (*Musa*), ginger lilies (*Hedychium*) and phormiums, as well as the world's essential cereal food plants. Even disregarding the science, these borders have transformed the area to the south-west of the house with strong forms and late-season colour.

In the Lower Garden, a subtropical border envelopes the lawn in front of this very English house, giving it echoes of Christopher Lloyd's garden at Great Dixter. Here, very poor sandy soil supports bottlebrushes (*Callistemon*), echiums, acanthus, sea hollies (*Eryngium*), bananas and palms. Feeling that the open grass was a little boring for visitors, the gardeners regularly mow a turf maze in this area.

Mottistone Gardens has moved to battery power for most of its machinery. The mowers and hedging shears now need less servicing, which is important on an island, and it means there is less noise and smell. Climate change is not just about using less water; the gardeners have found that, over the last decade, the rainfall has been more unpredictable – it comes in heavier bursts that can do more damage to plants. Fortunately, the monocots are proving to be quite robust.

At Mottistone, the history, the climate and the people have all come together to produce a very special place. The gardeners and regular volunteers who help to maintain it clearly love their work - so much so that the head gardener has never sought to work anywhere else. In 2005, twenty-five olive trees (*Olea europaea*) were planted by each one of the staff and volunteers. It was an experiment for the new century that is now paying off: every one of those olive trees is thriving. Looking back while looking forward is what Mottistone does best.

AGAPANTHUS

Agapanthus (sometimes called African lily) has been grown in Europe since the seventeenth century. Although agapanthus may look tender and exotic, it is actually a tough plant. In its native South Africa it anchors itself on the side of cliffs, so is used to wind. Its need for plenty of sunshine, warmth and good drainage makes it an ideal island plant.

Widely grown is the species *Agapanthus africanus* (an evergreen with dark blue flowers and narrow leaves) and its white version, *A. africanus* 'Albus'. Neither is particularly tall, at 45cm/18in, nor as showy as some of the newer cultivars, but both have a natural look and grow well in the borders at Mottistone and elsewhere on the Isle of Wight. Also evergreen are the myriad cultivars of *A. praecox* subsp. *orientalis*, which are available in every shade of white and blue. On the Isle of Wight, the Channel Islands and the Isles of Scilly, these plants thrive outdoors all year-round.

Other popular agapanthus are the semi-evergreen *A.* Headbourne hybrids, which, with climate change, gardeners are finding can now be left out throughout winter. Alternatively they can be grown in pots, because agapanthus like to have their roots restricted (as they would in a cliff crevice) to really flower well. The pots can be moved into a greenhouse or dry shed for winter.

Agapanthus praecox subsp. *orientalis*

Crab Cottage

It was a misty early summer morning in 1991 when Mencia Scott discovered what would become her island home in Newtown Creek. In addition to their London base, her husband, Peter, was looking for somewhere to be close to the sea for sailing and Mencia wanted to give wings to her interest in growing plants in more challenging conditions.

The 0.5-hectare/1¼-acre plot lay just 100m/110 yards from the inlet that connects the village of Shalfleet with the Solent. Long, thin and oval-shaped, the plot ran both north and south of the house, with the eighteenth-century cottage placed in the middle. The cottage may at one time have controlled the saltings – the area of land to the north that is regularly inundated by the tide.

Crab Cottage did not offer the best conditions for making a garden. The ground was covered with brambles and ground ivy, and the plot was surrounded with 70–80 elm (*Ulmus*) trees. There was only a thin layer of topsoil over gravel, so that retention of nutrients was difficult. Rabbits fed and scraped at will, while moles foraged widely for worms under the grass. The main threat was the south-westerly, salt-laden winds.

OPPOSITE: The eighteenth-century Crab Cottage once controlled the nearby saltings of Newtown Creek.
BELOW: The front of the house faces east and has been simply planted with clipped lollipops of *Pittosporum tenuifolium* and two large honey spurges (*Euphorbia mellifera*) either side of the door.

Nevertheless, the Scotts were heartened by the mildness of the winters, the number of warm, sunny days in summer (although it was often dry) and the good drainage.

The first priority was to establish shelter belts, particularly on the western boundary. However, this was during the time that the dreaded Dutch elm disease was threatening native trees. Believing assurances that the disease would be abated, the Scotts cut and laid the elms as hedges. It worked, but only for two or three years beyond the death of the standing elms. Eventually, all the elms had to be felled or grubbed out.

Now fully exposed to the winds, they planted an outer barrier of Leyland cypress (× *Cuprocyparis leylandii*) and a further barrier of bay laurel (*Laurus nobilis*), protected in its early years by green mesh barriers to diffuse the winds. On the eastern boundary, to create shelter from the north-easterlies of early spring, the Scotts established a mixed hedge of traditional hawthorn (*Crataegus*), dogwood (*Cornus*) and dog rose (*Rosa canina*), together with stretches of cherry laurel (*Prunus laurocerasus*), bay laurel and beech (*Fagus*).

THE MAKING OF A GARDEN

The next stage of the garden making was to use a digger to level the ground, particularly on the south side, closest to the cottage, and to build a wall across the narrow waist of the plot so that borders could be laid out on three sides.

On the north side of the cottage, a long, narrow croquet lawn was created, allowing views along the estuary to the Solent and to Beaulieu. Beyond the croquet lawn and, in contrast to its clipped neatness, a wild area of meadow was created on either side of a meandering path. This leads to a screen of sweet peas (*Lathyrus odoratus*) that fronts a mixed hedge and hides a wildlife pond, dug on a rare pocket of clay in this otherwise particularly porous soil.

With Mencia's increasing knowledge of plants, she and Peter also wanted to develop a formal, sheltered, Mediterranean-style garden in an area that had been an orchard with elderly cooking-apple trees, pines and long grass. Peter decided that some hard landscaping would be a good idea to create a variety of levels and provide interest. He also added as many paths

as possible, to allow close contact with the plants. A broad central path was laid, with borders coming off it to provide the backbone of the design, adding overhead frames to support white wisteria and climbing roses. A shallow pool was made in front of a Chinese-style pavilion, its lead roof curling up at the corners. The pool is clear with black-painted sides and bottom, designed for reflection rather than plants.

Within this sheltered enclosure, the planting shines with evergreen subshrubs. Lavender (*Lavandula*), myrtle (*Myrtus*), rosemary (*Rosmarinus*), sage (*Salvia*) and rock roses (*Cistus*) give echoes of southern France, while cabbage palms (*Cordyline*), cannas, dahlias, pineapple lilies (*Eucomis*), bananas (*Musa*), red hot pokers (*Kniphofia*) and alstroemerias suggest the southern hemisphere. These are interspersed with roses (always a challenge on poor soil), sedums, *Agapanthus* Headbourne hybrids and unusual trees and shrubs, such as the salt tree (*Halimodendron halodendron*) grown for its wonderful peeling bark, *Indigofera decora* and Chinese plumbago (*Ceratostigma willmottianum*).

GLOBAL INFLUENCES

As a planting description, 'Mediterranean' has to be used loosely at Crab Cottage. Born in Switzerland and bought up in the south of France, Mencia has also spent time in East Asia and South Africa, all of which have informed her plant choices. The garden is a vivid, eclectic mix of plants that obey no rules. Mencia was influenced not so much by a particular style of gardening as by a strain of adventurous gardeners including Alan Gray at the Old Vicarage, East Ruston in Norfolk and Nori and Sandra Pope, who formerly gardened at Hadspen in Somerset.

OPPOSITE: The neat croquet lawn leads down to a wilder area with views out to the estuary and across to the mainland.
ABOVE: The pool and pavilion area is planted with a global mix of southern-hemisphere and Mediterranean plants.
FOLLOWING PAGES: The south-facing enclosed garden at Crab Cottage offers a chance to grow a wide range of plants, from English roses to South African pineapple lilies. Dahlias and *Verbena bonariensis* add colourful accents.

The pavilion and pool neatly screen the working area of compost bins. The organic matter is vital to put back as many nutrients as possible into the soil. This is done by mulching (each autumn and again each spring) with home-made compost and extra manure from local stables.

CHALLENGE VERSUS OPPORTUNITY

There is, as in many gardens, a struggle between the formal and less formal areas. Mencia favours the latter: *Verbena bonariensis* floats across the sunny parts of the garden, and tobacco plants (*Nicotiana sylvestris* and *N. mutabilis*) light up the shady areas. Peter and the part-time gardener concentrate on keeping the croquet lawn sharply defined, the grass mowed and the topiary in trim. Holm oaks (*Quercus ilex*), osmanthus, *Griselinia littoralis*, *Olearia* × *haastii* and Japanese mock orange (*Pittosporum tobira*) are the evergreens of choice. Even these coastal stalwarts can get scorched by the salt gales that blow across the garden – the Scotts have many times come home to find that the trees and shrubs have been burnt – as if by a blow torch.

The challenges of salt winds and gales are common to many seaward gardens, but there are wonderful opportunities at Crab Cottage, too: to capture the view across the salt marshes to the creek, the Solent and beyond; to make the most of the fantastically well-drained soil and mild climate so that bananas, dahlias and cannas can be left *in situ* throughout winter; to embrace the sunny summers and fill the borders with tender plants and scented-leaved pelargoniums. The occasional air frost notwithstanding, these gardeners travel with hope, growing whatever they choose – even hungry feeders such as hostas and roses – and put failures down to experience.

BELOW: Narrow gravel paths give easy access to the plants.
OPPOSITE CLOCKWISE FROM TOP LEFT: *Dahlia* 'Peaches and Cream', *Dahlia* 'Jan van Schaffelaar', *Dahlia* 'Bright Eyes', *Eucomis comosa*, *Dahlia* 'Natal', *Dahlia* 'David Howard', *Dahlia* Happy Days Pink, *Canna* hybrid, *Lilium* Asiatic hybrid.

HOLY ISLAND

HOLY ISLAND LIES JUST 1.6 kilometres/1 mile off the east coast of Northumberland, by the shortest crossing point. Until the twelfth century it was known as Lindisfarne, and since then it has become a place of retreat, partly because of its tidal status - access is via a causeway, which is flooded twice a day, cutting the island off completely - and partly because of its ecclesiastical history. Its appeal has endured to this day for the thousands of pilgrims who come to visit the priory, the castle and one of the smallest gardens in Britain to have been designed by Gertrude Jekyll. Holy Island has also become a destination for birdwatchers and naturalists. Some 3,500 hectares/8,650 acres of the island, its mudflats and marine habitats are a National Nature Reserve managed by Natural England.

Home to monks, bishops and saints including St Cuthbert, Lindisfarne Priory's monastic story ended in the reign of King Henry VIII and the story of its castle began. Built to command a strategic position overlooking the harbour, by the twentieth century the castle had become a neglected place. Its restoration - and the story of its garden - begins in 1901, when Edward Hudson, founder of *Country Life* magazine, called in architect Sir Edwin Lutyens and his design partner Jekyll to convert the castle into a comfortable Edwardian country house and to create a garden for his guests.

PREVIOUS PAGES: Holy Island, off the coast of Northumberland, includes several tiny islets such as this one, known as St Cuthbert's Isle.
LEFT: Holy Island is connected to the mainland only at low tide.

Lindisfarne Castle

On a late spring morning in 1906, four men manoeuvred a rotund, bespectacled woman, carrying a suitcase of drawing materials, into a rowing boat to cross the water to Holy Island in Northumberland. It was the sixty-three-year-old Gertrude Jekyll, who, accompanied by architect Sir Edwin Lutyens, was paying her first visit to Lindisfarne Castle, at the request of its owner, *Country Life* magnate Edward Hudson. They had taken the train from Kings Cross to Belford (along with Lutyens's pet raven, Jack) and made the journey by horse and cart to the crossing point at Ross, not risking the narrow causeway with its dangerous and fluctuating tides.

Lutyens and Jekyll were already a celebrated design partnership and, while Lutyens was charged with making Hudson's house habitable, plans were also afoot for the castle grounds. These involved converting an old walled vegetable plot 500 metres/550 yards north of the castle into something that would look good from the Ship Room (which became the drawing room), and from the bedrooms being created in the upper floors. It became Jekyll's smallest garden design and her only work on an island.

PARTNERS AT WORK

Lutyens is reputed to have spent this joint visit trying to construct a cage for the raven - castles, he said, should have ravens - while Jekyll roamed the island with her sketchbook. The walled garden - a former livestock pen within Castle Field - was surrounded by high walls and was a considerable walk from the castle, where Hudson planned to entertain summer visitors. Lutyens had grandiose plans for landscaping the entire valley as a water garden, adding tennis courts and croquet lawns. Jekyll, it seemed, was more interested in the wild plants growing on the shore and on the craggy surface of Beblowe Craig, on which the castle stands. Unable to establish plants in the sheer rock face herself, she had an eight-year-old local boy (Harry Walker, who lived to tell

Jekyll and Lutyens's garden was designed to be viewed from the castle, especially from the Ship Room and Lower Battery.

ABOVE: Gertrude Jekyll peppered Beblowe Craig with seeds of red valerian and snow-in-summer, fired from a shotgun.

RIGHT: Upturned fishing boats were used as storage sheds on the shore.

OPPOSITE: As it was set some way from the castle in an old sheep enclosure, Lutyens and Jekyll worked hard to make the garden appear larger than it really was.

the tale) lowered down in a basket from the Upper Battery, to plant red valerian (*Centranthus ruber*), snow-in-summer (*Cerastium tomentosum*) and viper's bugloss (*Echium vulgare*) in the crevices. This method of planting was only partially successful, and Jekyll also had the muzzle of a shotgun loaded with balls of seeds, which were fired into the rock. The ancestors of those plants thrive today.

Yet, for all their enthusiasm for the project, neither Jekyll nor Lutyens was able to get on with the gardens. Converting a ruinous Tudor castle into an Arts & Crafts house had taken most of the budget and it was not until January 1911 that Lutyens was able to lower and contour the walls of the garden, the shape echoing the dips in the landscape. He laid out paths of uncut stone to strict rules of perspective, using converging lines and gradual reductions in the widths of both paths and borders, to make the garden 'widen' when viewed from the castle. Jekyll used this architectural plan as the basis for her two planting plans: one for the first year, consisting of vegetables with annuals for colour; and a more permanent scheme of shrubs and perennials with a reduced number of annuals, and a single border of herbs and vegetables.

There is no disguising the fact that this is a small garden - just 0.05 hectare/⅛ acre, although both architect and designer worked hard to make it appear larger. Lutyens played with perspective while Jekyll concentrated on colour choice - using blue at the front, for example, to make it look wider. She wasn't just planting pretty flowers. The vibrant colours and repeated plantings meant that for a visitor there was no 'rest', no settling - it was designed to be a garden to move through.

Lindisfarne Castle walled garden was also intended only as a summer garden, designed to reach full flowering in mid- and late summer. Jekyll tended to use mainly perennials in her planting schemes but there is clear evidence that at Lindisfarne Castle she used more annuals (see page 185). By late autumn, the annuals have been pulled out, the perennials cut back and the shrubs pruned. The garden literally is put to bed for the winter.

REDISCOVERY AND INTERPRETATION

Jekyll's involvement at Lindisfarne was almost forgotten until the 1970s, when former Durham University lecturer Michael Tooley (author with Rosanna Tooley of *The Gardens of Jekyll in Northern England*) tracked down the original plans, which had been auctioned a few years after Jekyll's death in 1932, and later deposited in the Beatrix Farrand archive at the University of California. Tooley's research, and subsequent work by the National Trust, which took over Lindisfarne Castle in 1944, have filled out what we now know as a complete and exciting example of Jekyll's approach to planting and colour theory. The plans themselves are almost illegible but they, informed by the educated guesses of some garden historians as to what was her usual practice, have enabled the National Trust to maintain and stock a garden close to how she had envisaged it.

The garden has had several long-standing, committed gardeners, who lead a small team of volunteers. Their work is not only shoehorned into the summer months, but must also take account of the high- and low-water timetable: on Holy Island, the window of low-tide crossing times dictates every activity, from shop opening times to gardening. At most, they have seven hours from arriving – or risk being stranded overnight. Despite the challenges, Lindisfarne Castle garden is still one of the most rewarding and unusual gardens in which to work anywhere in Britain.

OPPOSITE ABOVE: The view south from the castle is over the walled garden.
OPPOSITE BELOW LEFT: A stone plaque celebrates Gertude Jekyll's involvment in the garden between 1906 and 1912.
OPPOSITE BELOW RIGHT: Herringbone cobblestones were chosen for the entrance.
ABOVE: Sweet peas, grown on canes and obelisks, lift the eye out towards the sea.

JEKYLL'S THEORY IN PRACTICE

It goes without saying that a small tidal island off the coast of north-east England does not share the soils or climate of the southern counties where most of Jekyll's other clients lived (she did, in fact, make other gardens for Edward Hudson, including his home at the Deanery in Berkshire). This part of Northumberland is technically in a 'rain shadow', so rainfall is not particularly high. In addition, the wind dries any moisture very quickly, and the soil in the garden is light and free-draining - tending towards the alkaline. Nor does this garden suffer from the usual bane of island gardens - salt spray - since it is just physically too far from the sea. Gales, however, are commonplace and the wind whisks in and catches the corners of the beds, causing the sweet peas (*Lathyrus odoratus*) to lean precariously.

The planting in Lindisfarne Castle walled garden needed to be bold as it was intended to be visible from the castle - particularly from the Ship Room and the Lower and Upper Batteries. The strong lines drawn by Lutyens were marked out by Jekyll with grey-leaved *Stachys byzantina*, grown for its foliage. In Jekyll's day it would not have been allowed to flower, but these days it is given free rein, to encourage bees.

The east-facing bed was for roses such as *Rosa* 'Zéphirine Drouhin' and the recently discovered *R.* 'Killarney', of 1898. In the north-facing bed, where the seat offered views back to the castle, there was a mixed planting of fuchsias (*F. magellanica* and *F.* 'Riccartonii'), shrubs and perennials in a red and pink colour theme. Santolina planted next to the bench was intentionally placed to repel insects naturally. From the seat, the eye would take in Jekyll's borders of delphiniums, lavateras and hollyhocks (*Alcea*). She varied the heights of her yellow-spectrum plants with tall rudbeckias, shorter heleniums and lots of annual chrysanthemums in cream and yellow. Jekyll also specified the sweet peas at the corners of the beds - the newly bred *Lathyrus odoratus* 'Countess Spencer' (first shown in 1901), with its larger, wavy-petalled flowers, was one she particularly liked. She had it planted on hazel supports, which had to be carted in from the mainland.

LEFT FROM TOP: Jekyll chose *Scabiosa caucasica*, *Malus domestica* 'Ellison's Orange' and *Rudbeckia fulgida* var. *speciosa* for permanent planting.
RIGHT: Lutyens lowered the stone walls at the front of the garden to allow views to and from the castle.

The gardener's shed fits perfectly in one corner of the walled area.

The centrepiece of the garden was a sundial surrounded by stachys and infilled with *Sedum telephium* 'Munstead Red' (now known as *Hylotelephium telephium* 'Munstead Red'), one of Jekyll's own selections sent from her home at Munstead Wood in Surrey. This has proved reliable and now fills the centre of the garden, but other plants have proved unsuitable. Jekyll wanted delphiniums, but at Lindisfarne Castle they get slug damage so have been replaced with the less fussy annual larkspur *Consolida ajacis.* Hollyhocks and lavateras were two other Jekyll recommendations that didn't work as planned - the lavateras caught rust from the hollyhocks. The lavateras will stay, but the hollyhocks have had to be sacrificed. Likewise, the original roses succumbed to rose sickness and were all replaced - the team are now experimenting with some of the new, shorter English roses - including *Rosa* Gertrude Jekyll (a modern rose bred in the 1980s and named after her).

The original obelisks used to support *Clematis flammula* were rotten and have been replaced - and are now used to support a much wider range of old-fashioned sweet peas. Different heritage varieties are trialled each year, including *Lathyrus odoratus* 'Prince of Orange' (1928), *L.o.* 'Gwendoline' (one of the Spencer sweet peas) and *L.o* 'Henry Thomas'.

For many years it was thought that Jekyll advised vegetables to be grown only in the first year of the garden's life, but the National Trust now believes that she clearly planned a border of herbs, salads, vegetables and espalier fruit. Strawberries, sage, thyme, chives and French tarragon are all mentioned and now grow beneath newly planted espaliered apples that would have been available in the early twentieth century: 'Ellison's Orange' (1890) and 'Reverend W. Wilks' (1904).

Gertrude Jekyll gardens can appear relaxed and natural but, on the contrary, they are strictly planned. No self-seeding in the borders was (or is) allowed, although her one concession was to encourage plants to develop in the cracks between the paving - something the current gardeners will introduce more of over the coming years.

At the end of a working day, the turn of the tide acts like a silent bell, drawing people on to and off the island to their homes on either side of the water. Those lucky enough to stay on Holy Island overnight can experience the song of the seals - the eerie, unforgettable calls they make as they gather on the sandbanks waiting for the tide to reveal their own 'islands'. It is a sound that hasn't changed over the centuries and, like every visitor, Lutyens and Jekyll must have come under its spell.

GERTRUDE JEKYLL'S FLOWERING ANNUALS

When Gertrude Jekyll came to Lindisfarne in spring 1906 she was already a celebrated designer and plantswoman with many gardens to her name as well as her own at Munstead Wood in Surrey. Her painterly approach to colour in the borders inspired Edwardian and subsequent generations of gardeners to follow her theories.

The garden at Lindisfarne was an ideal opportunity for her to put into practice one of her key tenets: that the only way to create a good planting scheme was to 'devote certain borders to certain times of year, each border or region of the garden to be bright for from one to three months'. This was what she wrote in her book *Colour in the Flower Garden*, published when she was sixty-five during the period between her first visit to Lindisfarne and when the gardens were actually planted up. Lindisfarne was, in some ways, an experiment – how to keep a summer garden looking good from midsummer until early autumn.

One of the ways Jekyll did this was by including annual flowers. We tend to think of 'Jekyll gardens' as shining examples of the mixed and herbaceous borders, with annuals featuring occasionally. However, at Lindisfarne she gave them more prominence and suggested using annual sweet peas (she was normally a big advocate of the perennial sweet pea *Lathyrus latifolius*). She suggested mignonette (*Reseda odorata*), to be grown each year from seed for scent; mignonettes do not have striking flowers, so Jekyll was clearly thinking of the perfume, perhaps motivated by her own failing eyesight. The other annual she favoured was *Chrysanthemum coronarium* (now *Glebionis coronaria*) for its range of yellows and creams. For blues she used the annual cornflower *Centaurea cyanus* as well as the plant Jekyll knew as love-in-a-mist (*Nigella damascena*). The cultivar *N.d.* 'Miss Jekyll' that was named after her is now grown in the garden at Lindisfarne.

Lathyrus odoratus 'Gwendoline'   *Lathyrus odoratus* 'Henry Thomas'   *Glebionis coronaria*

Glebionis coronaria 'Primrose Gem'   *Centaurea cyanus*   *Nigella damascena* 'Miss Jekyll'

Travel and Garden Guide

For this book, the author and photographer took thirty-eight boats and ferries, two plane journeys, crossed three bridges and two tidal causeways (each), travelling approximately 12,000 kilometres/7,450 miles by car and a few less on foot. Here's some practical advice if you want to follow part or all of their journey.

The following is a guide only, and travel arrangements and garden opening times should be checked on the websites before setting off. This is particularly important for islands, where weather conditions and transport can change at short notice. All details were correct at the time of publication, but please let the publishers know if the information is incorrect and they will update it in the next edition.

THE ISLES OF SCILLY

Lying 45 kilometres/28 miles from Cornwall, Scilly can be reached by plane from some UK airports, or by the Scillonian ferry via Penzance (www.islesofscilly-travel.co.uk). The ferry crossing takes less than three hours and goes to the largest island, St Mary's. From there, small boats can take you across to the other islands of Tresco, Bryher, St Martin's and St Agnes; tickets can be bought on the quay at St Mary's Harbour. The boatmen rule the waves here; because the seas around Scilly are very shallow, the tide times have to be strictly adhered to. Taking a car to any of the islands is prohibitively expensive unless you are resident. Taxis and buses operate on St Mary's.

TRESCO
The island (www.tresco.co.uk) can be visited for the day from the other islands, but it also has cottage accommodation, as well as pubs and hotels. Transport is by bike or electric buggy; no cars are allowed.

Tresco Abbey Garden, Tresco, TR24 0QQ (www.tresco.co.uk/enjoying/abbey-garden); open daily year-round.

Tresco Abbey Garden: A Personal and Pictorial History by Mike Nelhams (Curator) (Truran, 2nd edn 2015) is the best book on the gardens.

WORTH NOTING ON OTHER ISLANDS
The daffodil growers at Churchtown Farm, St Martin's, TR25 0QL (www.scillyflowers.co.uk).
Polreath garden, tea room and guesthouse, Higher Town, St Martin's, TR25 0QL (www.polreath.com)
Scented Narcissi represents farms growing flowers on St Agnes and St Mary's (www.scentednarcissi.co.uk).
Carreg Dhu Community Garden, St Mary's TR21 0NW (www.scillyonline.co.uk/carreg.html)

THE SOUTH-WESTERN ISLES OF SCOTLAND

This is not one journey but several, although if you want to follow in the author's footsteps the starting point is Wemyss Bay, south-west of Glasgow. For the gardens, go to www.gardens-of-argyll.co.uk/.

ARRAN

From the mainland, the main ferry is from the port of Ardrossan. Catch the Arran ferry (www.calmac.co.uk) which lands at Brodick, close to Brodick Castle. The northern sea approach to Arran from the Kintyre peninsula is to Lochranza.

Brodick Castle Garden and Country Park, Brodick, Isle of Arran, KA27 8HY (www.nts.org.uk/Visit/Brodick-Castle-and-Country-Park); the country park is open daily year-round while the garden is open on varying days of the year.

BUTE

From Wemyss Bay the ferry (www.calmac.co.uk) goes almost hourly to Bute, landing in Rothesay, which is convenient for all gardens there.

Ascog Hall, Ascog, Isle of Bute, PA20 9EU (www.ascogfernery.com); open daily from Easter to October.

OTHER PLACES ON BUTE MENTIONED IN CHAPTER 2
Mount Stuart, Isle of Bute, PA20 9LR (www.mountstuart.com); open daily from April to October; tours of the house need to be booked.
Ardencraig Gardens, Ardencraig Lane, High Craigmore, Rothesay, Isle of Bute, PA20 9EZ (www.gardens-of-argyll.co.uk/view-details.php?id=471); open daily from May to September.

Bute by David McDowall (The Laird Press, 2010) is a comprehensive history and guide to the island.

GIGHA

The Isle of Gigha lies off the west coast of Kintyre and is accessed by boat (www.calmac.co.uk) from the crossing place at Tayinloan. The crossing to Gigha takes only 20 minutes. The Isle of Gigha Heritage Trust website (www.gigha.org.uk) has information on everything you need to know about staying on the island and activities there.

Achamore Gardens, Achamore House, Isle of Gigha, PA41 7AD (www.gigha.org.uk/viewItem.php?id=8845&sectionTitle=Attractions); open daily year-round.

'Kitty Lloyd Jones: Lady Gardener and Nurserywoman' by Rachel Berger with Mary and Jenny Burns, *Garden History*, Vol. 25, No. 1 (Summer, 1997), pages 107-116, is a definitive account of her work.

ANGLESEY

Anglesey can be reached over one of two bridges: by road over the Menai Suspension Bridge; or by road or rail over the Britannia Bridge. The station is at Llanfairpwll.

Plas Cadnant, Cadnant Road, Menai Bridge, Isle of Anglesey, North Wales, LL59 5NH (www.plascadnant.co.uk/2/en-GB/THE-HIDDEN-GARDENS); open on varying days from April to October; at other times by appointment. The owner (and head gardener) also leads regular guided tours and groups are welcome by appointment. There are several holiday cottages within the grounds, with their own private gardens and courtyards.

OTHER PLACES MENTIONED IN CHAPTER 3
Plas Newydd House and Gardens, Llanfairpwll, Anglesey, LL61 6DQ (www.nationaltrust.org.uk/plasnewydd).

ORKNEY

Travel to Orkney is by plane from a variety of destinations or by ferry from Aberdeen to Kirkwall (www.northlinkferries.co.uk) or from Caithness: Scrabster to Stromness (www.northlinkferries.co.uk) or from Gill's Bay to St Margaret's Hope (www.pentlandferries.co.uk). From May to September, foot passengers can also travel from John O'Groats to Burwick, South Ronaldsay (www.jogferry.co.uk/Ferry.aspx). There are ferries between the various Orkney islands (www.orkneyferries.co.uk). For further information, including on accommodation, go to www.visitorkney.com/.

The Orkney Garden Trail includes gardens on South Ronaldsay, Mainland and Hoy and takes place very two years. The next one is scheduled for 2019; for details go to www.orkneygardentrail.org.uk/. Some of these gardens also open occasionally for charity under the Scotland's Gardens scheme (www.scotlandsgardens.org).

The updated edition of *Orkney: A Historical Guide* by Caroline Wickham-Jones (Birlinn, 2015) is a good introduction to the archaeology of Orkney.

MAINLAND

The Quoy of Houton, Orphir, Orkney, KW17 2RD (www.orkneybedandbreakfast.org.uk); the garden is open for guests and for other visitors by appointment. Garden entrance money is donated to the Friends of the Neuro Ward, Aberdeen Royal Infirmary. Also open for the Scotland's Gardens scheme. The owner, Caroline Critchlow, is the organizer of the biennial Orkney Garden Trail and also has holiday accommodation and offers drystone walling tuition year-round.

Kierfiold House, Sandwick, Orkney, KW16 3JE (www.kierfiold.co.uk); the garden is open for guests and for other visitors by appointment. Also open for the Scotland's Gardens scheme and for the Orkney Garden Trail. There is holiday cottage accommodation there, too.

SOUTH RONALDSAY

Fiddlers Green garden opens for the Orkney Garden Trail.

OTHER ORKNEY GARDENS OPEN ON A REGULAR BASIS
Firth Community Garden, Finstown, Mainland; and Marengo Community Garden, St Margaret's Hope, South Ronaldsay. Other private gardens including Stenwood in Finstown appear regularly on BBC Scotland's long-running gardening television programme *The Beechgrove Garden*. Some of these gardens also open occasionally for charity under the Scotland's Gardens scheme.

CHANNEL ISLANDS

Travel to Guernsey is by plane from a variety of destinations or by ferry from Portsmouth or Poole, Dorset, to St Peter Port (www.condorferries.co.uk). Guernsey and the two islands lying closest to it - Herm and Sark - may be explored together in a week or more. A good place to learn about the natural history of the islands and the native flora is La Société Guernesiaise (www.societe.org.gg) whose offices are in Candie Gardens in the main town of St Peter Port. For further information, including on accommodation, go to www.visitguernsey.com/.

GUERNSEY

La Bigoterie, Berthelot Street, St Peter Port, GY1 1JS; open by appointment and for scheduled Floral Guernsey charity openings (www.floralguernsey.co.uk).

OTHER PLACES ON GUERNSEY MENTIONED IN CHAPTER 5
Candie Gardens, St Peter Port, GY1 1DA (www.museums.gov.gg/candiegardens); home to some of the oldest heated glasshouses in the British Isles (*c*.1793) as well as a restored Victorian flower garden - with a café housed in the nineteenth-century bandstand. It is also the location for the annual nerine floral festival organised by Plant Heritage Guernsey (www.nccpgguernsey.co.uk).

HERM

Herm is a short passenger ferry ride from St Peter Port and tickets can be purchased on the esplanade (www.traveltrident.com). No cars are allowed on the island. For more information, go to www.herm.com/.

Herm Island Ltd, GY1 3HR; the gardeners run guided tours every Tuesday from mid-April to mid-September, starting at 11 a.m. from the harbour.

SARK

Sark is accessed by boat from St Peter Port (www.sarkshippingcompany.com); no cars are allowed. In summer, it is worth booking the ferry in advance; the crossing takes just under an hour. It is an uphill walk from Creux harbour (one of the smallest harbours in the world) to La Seigneurie Gardens, but there is tractor transport for anyone who needs it. Once in the 'centre', there are horses and carts offering tours of the island. For further information on travel and accommodation, go to www.sark.co.uk/.

La Seigneurie Gardens, Sark, GH10 1SF (www.laseigneuriegardens.com); open daily from Easter to October.

INNER HEBRIDES

MULL

Travel to Mull is by sea from a number of ports (www.calmac.co.uk) on the Scottish mainland. The main route is from Oban to Craignure, but the author travelled from farther north, from Kilchoan on the Ardamurchan Peninsula to Tobermory. There is also a crossing point at Lochaline for Fishnish. You can take a car to Mull, but the roads are mainly narrow, so allow plenty of time to cross the island.

Lip na Cloiche, Ballygown, nr Ulva Ferry, PA73 6LU (www.lipnacloiche. co.uk); open daily year-round. As well as running the garden and nursery, Lucy Mackenzie makes and sells artworks and offers bed and breakfast.

ORONSAY

Oronsay is managed by the RSPB (www.rspb.org.uk). It lies to the south of Colonsay and is linked to it by a tidal causeway, meaning that Oronsay can be accessed only on foot at low tide - usually for a two-hour window, twice a day. It is essential to consult the safe crossing timetable; tide timetables are posted at the CalMac office and in local shops etc. on Colonsay, which is reached by boat from Oban (www. calmac.co.uk) on the west coast of mainland Scotland. It is a two-hour sailing, often accompanied by porpoises, whales and dolphins.

The island offers a wide range of accommodation from hotels to hostels; see www.colonsay.org.uk/. Colonsay House has a garden café and its informal woodland garden is home to a spectacular rhododendron collection.

The Priory Garden on Oronsay is private and not open to the public. However, visitors can walk right up to the priory and view St Cuthbert's Cross and an unrivalled range of ancient stone monuments. For information about the birds and flora on Oronsay, go to www.rspb.org.uk/reserves-and-events/find-a-reserve/reserves-a-z/reserves-by-name/o/oronsay/.

SEIL

Lying some 20 kilometres/12 miles south of Oban, the Isle of Seil is an often-overlooked part of Scotland's west coast. It is linked to the mainland by the Atlantic Bridge (more correctly known as the Clachan bridge) on the B844.

An Cala, Isle of Seil, Argyll, PA34 4RF (www.gardens-of-argyll.co.uk/view-details.php?id=447); open daily from April to October. It is situated at the far end of the island in the village of Ellenabeich.

OTHER PLACES MENTION IN CHAPTER 6
Skye gets extremely busy in summer, and the authorities have been known to turn back visitors at the bridge if they do not have reserved accommodation. For further information, go to www.skye.co.uk/. Dunvegan Castle, Skye, IV55 8WF (www.dunvegancastle.com) sits at the north-west of the island; open daily from April to October. Armadale Castle, Armadale, Sleat, Skye, IV45 8RS (www.clandonald. com) lies in the south-west, close to the ferry crossing to Mull; open daily from April to October.

ISLE OF WIGHT

Car and passenger ferries cross daily from Southampton and Portsmouth to the Isle of Wight. For the gardens featured in this book, the Lymington (Hampshire) to Yarmouth (Isle of Wight) crossing is the most convenient (www.wightlink.co.uk.). For further information, including on accommodation, go to www.visitisleofwight.co.uk/.

Mottistone Gardens, Mottistone, near Brighstone, PO30 4ED (www. nationaltrust.org.uk/mottistone-gardens); gardens open daily year-round, but the house is open on only one or two days per year.

Crab Cottage, Mill Road, Shalfleet, PO30 4NE; open for visitors by appointment between May and September. Also open for charity under the National Gardens Scheme (www.ngs.org.uk).

OTHER PLACES MENTIONED IN CHAPTER 7
Osborne, York Avenue, East Cowes, PO32 6JX (www.english-heritage. org.uk/visit/places/osborne); open on varying days most of the year. Island home of Queen Victoria and Prince Albert with replanted parterres and productive walled garden.

HOLY ISLAND

Although Gertrude Jekyll arrived by boat, the normal way to travel to Holy Island is by road or on foot, crossing the causeway from the mainland east coast some 16 kilometres/10 miles south of Berwick-upon-Tweed. This is one of the most dangerous crossings for walkers or vehicle drivers who do not abide by the tide timetable. Every week, the rescue services have to go to the aid of someone who has been caught out by the rising water. Safe crossing times are clearly displayed online (http://orawww.northumberland.gov.uk/www2/holyisland/HolyIsland.asp) and on the island.

It is possible to visit for the day, although with an approximately five-hour 'window' of tides it is worth staying at one of the pubs, bed and breakfasts or self-catering accommodation. Also, the island is often very busy with day visitors, but less so in the evenings. For information on accommodation, retreats, walking and wildlife, go to www.lindisfarne.org.uk/.

Lindisfarne Castle, Holy Island, Berwick-upon-Tweed, Northumberland, TD15 2SH (www.nationaltrust.org.uk/lindisfarne); the garden is open daily year-round but the castle has more restricted opening times so check the website for details. The Jekyll garden is situated a short walk from the castle and looks its best in summer.

OTHER PLACES MENTIONED IN CHAPTER 8
Lindisfarne Priory, Holy Island, Berwick-Upon-Tweed, Northumberland, TD15 2RX (www.english-heritage.org.uk/visit/places/lindisfarne-priory).

Index

Page numbers in *italics* indicate a caption to an illustration.

abutilon 150
acacia 19
Acaena saccaticupula 'Blue Haze' 136
acanthus 163
Acer (maple) *49*
    A. palmatum (Japanese maple) 149
        A.p. 'Atropurpureum' *49*
    A. pseudoplatanus (sycamore) 54, *68*, 90, 111, 121
Achamore Gardens 29, 35, 40, 50–5, 186
Aconitum napellus (monkshood) 95, 136
Aeonium 19, *23*, 30, 104
    A. arboreum 'Atropurpureum' *30*
    A. canariense 30
Aesculus hippocastanum (horse chestnut) 54
African daisy *see Arctotis*
African lily *see Agapanthus*
Agapanthus (African lily) 15, *15*, 19, 30, 108, *157*, *162*, 163
    A. africanus 160, *161*, 163
        A.a. 'Albus' 163
    A. Headbourne hybrids 163, 167
    A. praecox subsp. *orientalis 1*, 163, *163*
agave 21, 39, 108
Alcea (hollyhock) 182, 184
Alchemilla mollis (lady's mantle) 82, 90, *93*
Alderney, Island of 98
Alexander-Sinclair, James 35
Allan, Malcolm 52, 54
Allium 82
    A. ampeloprasum 111
        A.a. var. *babingtonii* (Babington's leek) 15, 111
    A. hollandicum 'Purple Sensation' 66
    A. triquetrum 111
almond *see Prunus dulcis*
Aloe 21, *23*, 26
    A. polyphylla 30
alpine gardens *93*
alstroemeria 108, 167
An Cala 144–51, 188
Anemone x *hybrida* (Japanese anemone) 90
Anglesey (Ynys Môn) 9, 56–73, 186–7
annuals 185
Antirrhinum (snapdragon) 158
apothecary's rose *see Rosa gallica* var. *officinalis*
Appledore 7
apples 106, *106*, 111, 140, 158, 184; *see also Malus*
aquilegia *84*
Aralia racemosa 130
Araucaria
    A. araucana (monkey puzzle) 26, 44, *44*
    A. heterophylla (Norfolk Island pine) 11, 26, 108
Arctotis (African daisy) 160, *161*
Ardencraig Gardens 35, 186
Ardkinglas 52
Argyranthemum hybrid *30*
Armadale Castle 125, *125*, 188
Armeria maritima (sea pink) *11*
Arran, Isle of 11, 35, *35*, 36–42, 186
arum lily *see Zantedeschia aethiopica*
Ascog Hall 43–9, 186
astelia 163
aster 66, 158
astilbe 90, 150
Astilboides tabularis 130
astrantia 84, 90, 150
azalea 70, 114, 149

Babington's leek *see Allium ampeloprasum* var. *babingtonii*
bamboo 163
banana *see Musa*
Bannatyne Stewart, Alexander 43
Basford, John 36
Bateman, Edward La Trobe 43, *46*
bay laurel *see Laurus nobilis*
beachcomb finds *134*
beans, runner 106
Beatrix Farrand archive 181
Beaumont, Christopher 113
Beaumont, Michael and Diana 113, 114, *115*, 118, 121
Beblowe Craig 177, *178*
beech 35, 165
    southern *see Nothofagus*
Beechgrove Garden, The 82, 187
bees 111, 143, 182
bell heather *see Erica cinerea*
Bermuda buttercup *see Oxalis pes-caprae*
Beschorneria yuccoides 30
Betula (birch) 15, 54
Bigoterie, La 103–8, 187
bilberry 35
birch *see Betula*
Birch, Jo 118
bistort, common *see Persicaria bistorta*
blackthorn *see Prunus spinosa*
Blakeney, Captain and Mrs 149
bluebell *54*, 70
blueberry 114
Bodnant 53
Boscawen, Major J.P.T. 36, 39
bottlebrush *see Callistemon*
box *see Buxus*
Bremner, Alan 82, 91
bridges *11*, *30*
British Pteridological Society 48
Brodick Castle *35*, 36–42, 52, 186
Bryher, Island of 15
buckler fern *see Dryopteris*
Buddleja
    B. loricata 130
    B. salviifolia 130
Burke, Karin and Michael 44, 48
bush echium *see Echium candicans*
Butchart, Jennie 9
Bute, Isle of 35, 43–9, 186
Bute, 3rd Marquess of 35
buttercup, Bermuda *see Oxalis pes-caprae*
Buxus (box) 62, 104

cabbage tree *see Cordyline australis*
Caldey Island 11
Californian tree poppy *see Romneya coulteri*
Callistemon (bottlebrush) 163
camellia 40, 103, 104, 114
Campanula 84
    C. lactiflora 'Pritchard's Variety' 66
Canary Island 22
Canary Island date palm *see Phoenix canariensis*
Candie Gardens 100, *101*, 187
canna 106, *162*, 163, 167, 170
    hybrid *170*
Cardiocrinum giganteum (Himalayan lily) 70, *71*, 71
Carex (sedge) 35
    C. morrowii 95
Carpinus (hornbeam) 111, 158
Carreg Dhu Community Garden 186
Ceanothus cyaneus 130
Celli, Faith 146
Centaurea cyanus (cornflower) *118*, 185, *185*

Centranthus (valerian) 84
    C. ruber (red valerian) *178*, 179
Cerastium tomentosus (snow-in-summer) *178*, 179
Ceratostigma willmottianum 167
Cerinthe major 84
Channel Islands 96–121, 163, 187
cherry laurel *see Prunus laurocerasus*
chestnut, horse *see Aesculus*
Chilean fire bush *see Embothrium coccineum*
Chilean lantern tree *see Crinodendron hookerianum*
Chilean puya *see Puya chilensis*
Choisya ternata 19
Chrysanthemum 182
    C. coronarium see Glebionis coronaria
Chusan palm *see Trachycarpus fortunei*
ciob *see Molinia caerulea*
Cistus (rock rose) 167
Clachan Bridge *11*
Clematis 98, 132
    C. flammula 184
Clethra arborea (lily-of-the-valley tree) 39
Clifford, Rosamund 118
clivia 19, 21
Clough, Peter 29, 54
cobnut *see Corylus avellana*
Colburn, Ike W. and Frannie 138–40
Colonsay, Isle of 138, 143, 188
Colonsay House 52, 188
Colour in the Flower Garden 185
common spotted orchid *see Dactylorhiza fuchsii*
Consolida ajacis (larkspur) 184
Constance, Lake 9
Cordyline 44, *115*
    C. australis (cabbage tree) 26, 39, 167
        C.a. Purpurea Group *30*
    C. banksii 39
    C. indivisa 39
cornflower *see Centaurea cyanus*
Cornus (dogwood) 165
Cortaderia (pampas grass) 163
Corylus avellana (cobnut) 106
cosmos 104, 158
Cotoneaster horizontalis 149
Country Life 175, 177
crab apples *see Malus*
Crab Cottage 165–71, 188
cranesbill *see Geranium*
    dusky *see Geranium phaeum*
Crarae 52
Crataegus (hawthorn) 35, 165
Crinodendron 40
    C. hookerianum (Chilean lantern tree) 48, *49*
Critchlow, Caroline and Kevin 79–82
crocosmia 30, 82, 90
croquet lawn 165, *167*
Cupressus macrocarpa (Monterey cypress) 20
x *Cuprocyparis leylandii* (Leyland cypress) 165
Cydonia oblonga (quince) 106
cypress *see Cupressus*
    Leyland *see* x *Cuprocyparis leylandii*

Dactylorhiza
    D. fuchsii (common spotted orchid) 143
    D. maculata (heath spotted orchid) 143, *143*
daffodil *see Narcissus*
Dahlia 66, 104, 160, *161*, *167*, 167, 170
    D. 'Bishop of Llandaff' 106
    D. 'Bright Eyes' *170*
    D. 'David Howard' *170*
    D. Happy Days Pink *170*
    D. 'Jan van Schaffelaar' *170*
    D. 'Natal' *170*
    D. 'Peaches and Cream' *170*

daisy, African *see Arctotis*
damson 106
dandelion tree *see Sonchus arboreus*
Daphniphyllum macropodum 132
Darmera peltata 130, *131*, 150
datura 19
day lily *see Hemerocallis*
delphinium 182
Dianthus (pink) 16, *118*, 160
dicentra 84, 150
Digitalis (foxglove) 66, 82, 104
    D. purpurea 98
        D.p. f. *albiflora* 82
Diphylleia cymosa 130
disporum 130
dog rose *see Rosa canina*
dogwood *see Cornus*
Dorrien-Smith, Commander Tom *28*, 29
Dorrien-Smith, Lucy *26*
Dorrien-Smith, Major A.A. 20
Dorrien-Smith, Robert A. 21
Dorrien-Smith, Thomas Algernon 20
Douglas, David 48
Douglas fir *see Pseudotsuga menziesii*
Downie, Sheila 149, 150
Drimys winterii (winter's bark) 48
Dryopteris (buckler fern) 70
du Gard Pasley, Anthony 103
Dunvegan Castle 125, *125*, 188
Dutch elm disease 165

Easdale, Island of 145
East Ruston 167
Echinops (globe thistle) 95
Echium 10, 15, 22, *29*, 163
    E. candicans (bush echium/pride of Madeira) 10–11, 22, *22*, 136
    E. pininana (giant tree echium) 15–16, 22, *22*, 30, 108, 136
    E. x *scilloniensis* 22
    E. vulgare (viper's bugloss) 22, 179
Eden Project 30
Edinburgh Royal Botanic Garden 26, 43–4, 48, 53
Eilean Musdile *7*
Ellenbeich 146
elm *see Ulmus*
Eltham Palace 158
Elwes, Henry John 100
Embothrium coccineum (Chilean fire bush) 39, 48, 47
Erica cinerea (bell heather) 143, *143*
Erigeron karvinskianus *118*, *121*, *157*
Eryngium (sea holly) 163
Escallonia 17, 82
    E. macrantha 130, *131*
    E. rubra var. *macrantha* 90
eucalyptus 108
Eucomis comosa (pineapple lily) *167*, *167*, 170
euonymus 17
Eupatorium purpureum 66
Euphorbia mellifera (honey spurge) 30, *165*
Euryops chrysanthemoides 160
Evans, Huw and Sarah 103–7
Exbury 53
Exochorda x *macrantha* 'The Bride' 111

Fanning-Evans, Elizabeth 62
Fascicularia bicolor 95
Fermain Valley Hotel *98*, 100
ferneries 43, *46*, 47, 70, *70*, *131*
Fforde, Lady Jean 39
Fiddlers Green 84–5, 187
fig 106, 140
filipendula *148*, 150

Firth Community Garden 187
Fish, Margery 91
Forrest, George 36
foxglove see Digitalis
Fuchsia 104
    F. magellanica 90, 130, 182
    F. 'Riccartonii' 35, 182
Furcraea
    F. longaeva see F. parmentieri
    F. parmentieri 108, 111
Fyfe family 44

Gabs of May 84
Galanthus (snowdrop) 70
Gardeners' Chronicle 43, 47
gazebos 26
Geranium (cranesbill) 66, 82, 84, 87, 91, 93,
    95, 132
    G. x antipodeum 'Sea Spray' 91
    G. x cantabrigiense
        G. x c. 'St Ola' 82, 91
        G. x c. 'Westray' 91, 93
    G. clarkei
        G.c. 'Kashmir Purple' 95, 132
        G.c. 'Kashmir White' 91
    G. endressii x G. psilostemon see
        G. Patricia ('Brempat')
    G. 'Johnson's Blue' 82
    G. maderense 10, 11, 19, 29, 140
    G. x magnificum 91, 91
    G. nodosum 91
    G. orientalibeticum 91
    G. 'Orion' 132
    G. 'Orkney Blue' 91
    G. 'Orkney Pink' 91
    G. x oxonianum 'A.T. Johnson' 91, 91
    G. palmatum 136
    G. Patricia ('Brempat') 82, 91, 91
    G. phaeum (dusky cranesbill) 82
    G. pratense var. pratense f. albiflorum 91
    G. psilostemon 136
    G. Rozanne 104
    G. 'Storm Chaser' 91
giant tree echium see Echium pininana
Gigha, Isle of 11, 35, 40, 50–5, 186
ginger lily see Hedychium
Gladiolus communis subsp. byzantinus 15,
    92, 93, 95
glasshouses 43, 46, 114, 136, 137
Glebionis coronaria 185, 185
    G.c. 'Primrose Gem' 185
Glendoick 52
globe thistle see Echinops
Goat Fell 35
gorse 11, 15, 35
Graham, James Gillespie 36
Gran Canaria 11
grapes 98, 140
Gray, Alan 167
Great Dixter 163
greengages 106
Griselinia littoralis 39–40, 106, 140, 170
    G.l. 'Variegata' 130
Guernsey, Island of 98–101, 103–8, 187
Guernsey lily see Nerine sarniensis
Gunnera manicata 40

Hadspen 167
Halimodendron halodendron (salt tree) 167
Hamilton, Duke of 36
Hamilton, Lady Marie Louise see Montrose,
    Duchess of
Hathaway, Sibyl 113
hawthorn see Crataegus
heath 15
heather 35
    bell see Erica cinerea
    Cape 29
Hebe 19, 140
    H. pinguifolia 'Pagei' 140
    H. salicifolia 132
    H. 'White Wand' 136

Hebrides 11
    Inner 122–51, 187–8
    Outer 35, 125
hedges 10, 16, 17, 62, 90, 104, 106, 108, 118,
    130, 131, 140, 140, 157
Hedychium (ginger lily) 108, 163
helenium 182
helichrysum 30
Heligan, Lost Gardens of 62
Hemerocallis (day lily) 161
herbaceous borders 66, 95, 160
Herm, Island of 22, 98, 108–11, 187
Herston 84
heuchera 106
hibiscus 104
Himalayan honeysuckle see Leycesteria
    formosa
Himalayan lily see Cardiocrinum giganteum
Historic Scotland 43
Hobhouse, Penelope 138, 140
holly 35
    sea see Eryngium
hollyhock see Alcea
holm oak see Quercus ilex
Holy Island 172–85, 188
honeysuckle see Lonicera
Hordeum jubatum 118
Horlick, Sir James 40, 50–4
hornbeam see Carpinus
horse chestnut see Aesculus hippocastanum
Hudson, Edward 175, 177, 182
Huntingdon Botanic Garden 26
Hydrangea 70, 104, 114
    H. arborescens 'Annabelle' 150
    H. aspera 132
        H.a. Villosa Group 150
    H. macrophylla 106
        H.m. 'Madame Emile Mouillère' 150

Indigofera decora 167
Inner Hebrides 122–51, 187–8
Instrahull, Island of 138
Inula magnifica 130
Inverewe 52
Iona, Isle of 11, 138
Ipomoea (morning glory) 111
Isle of Gigha Heritage Trust 54
Isle of Wight see Wight, Isle of

Jacob's ladder see Polemonium
Japanese anemone see Anemone x hybrida
Japanese cherry see Prunus serrulata
Japanese maple see Acer palmatum
Japanese mock orange see Pittosporum
    tobira
Japanese snowbell see Styrax japonica
Jekyll, Gertrude 66, 140, 175–84, 177, 185
Jersey, Island of 98
Juglans (walnut) 103
Juniperus (juniper) 158

Kierfiold House 87–95, 187
king fern see Todea barbara
Kingdon-Ward, Frank 36, 53
Kintyre peninsula 35
Kirstenbosch National Botanic Garden 26
Kniphofia (red hot poker) 108, 162, 163, 167

La Seigneurie Gardens Trust 114, 121
laburnum 54
lady's mantle see Alchemilla mollis
lampranthus 108
Landsborough, Rev. David 11
larkspur see Consolida ajacis
Lathyrus
    L. latifolius (perennial sweet pea) 185
    L. odoratus (sweet pea) 68, 104, 118, 165,
        181, 182
        L.o. 'Countess Spencer' 182
        L.o. 'Gwendoline' 184, 185, 185
        L.o. 'Henry Thomas' 184, 185, 185
        L.o. 'Prince of Orange' 184

laurel
    bay see Laurus nobilis
    cherry see Prunus laurocerasus
Laurus nobilis (bay laurel) 36, 165
Lavandula 167
    L. angustifolia 'Munstead' 160
lavatera 182, 184
Lawson, Andrew 21
Le Manoir 108, 111
Leichtlin, Max 100
Leucospermum 108
    L. cordifolium 30
Leycesteria formosa (Himalayan
    honeysuckle)) 48
Leyland cypress see x Cuprocyparis leylandii
libertia 82, 90
lighthouses 7–9
Ligularia 'Britt Marie Crawford' 130
Ligustrum ovalifolium (privet) 108, 140,
    140, 157
Lilium Asiatic hybrid (lily) 170
lily see Lilium
    African see Agapanthus
    arum see Zantedeschia aethiopica
    day lily see Hemerocallis
    ginger see Hedychium
    Guernsey see Nerine sarniensis
    Himalayan see Cardiocrinum giganteum
    pineapple see Eucomis
    water see Nymphaea
lily-of-the-valley tree see Clethra arborea
lime see Tilia 35
Lindisfarne 11; see also Holy Island
Lindisfarne Castle 175–85, 188
Lindisfarne Priory 175, 188
Lip Na Cloiche 126–37, 188
Lismore lighthouse 7
Lloyd, Christopher 163
Lloyd Jones, Kitty 52, 187
Lobb brothers 71
Lochranza 52
Logan Botanical Garden 26
Lonicera (honeysuckle) 95, 142
loosestrife see Lysimachia
love-in-a-mist see Nigella damascena
Lupinus (lupin) 82, 84
    L. arboreus (tree lupin) 16
Lutyens, Edwin 157–8, 175–9, 177
Lysimachia (loosestrife) 95
    L. punctata 95, 148, 150

machair 11, 142, 143
Mackenzie, Compton 108
Mackenzie Panizzon, Lucy 128, 131, 131,
    132, 188
Mackintosh, Charles Rennie 50
MacNeill, Malcolm 52
magnolia 40, 49
Mainau Island 9
Maitland, Charles 114
Malus (apple/crab apple) 106, 158
    M. 'Ellison's Orange' 182, 184
    M. 'Reverend W. Wilks' 184
maple see Acer
Marengo Community Garden 187
Marie of Baden, Princess 36
Mason, Maurice 26
Mawson, Thomas 35, 146, 146, 149, 151
maze 118, 162
Meconopsis 130
    M. (Fertile Blue Group) 'Lingholm' 49
Mediterranean stone pine see Pinus pinea
medlar see Mespilus germanica
Medwyns of Anglesey 62
Melbourne Royal Botanic Gardens 43
Menzies, Archibald 48
mesembryanthemum 23, 111
Mespilus germanica (medlar) 106, 106, 140
Metrosideros excelsa (New Zealand
    Christmas tree) 26
mignonette see Reseda odorata
mimulus 150

Miscanthus sinensis
    M.s. 'Variegatus' 82
    M.s. 'Zebrinus' 163
mock orange, Japanese see Pittosporum
    tobira
Moinerie, La 113
Molinia caerulea (purple moor grass) 35
monkey puzzle see Araucaria araucana
monkshood see Aconitum
monocotyledon plants 160–3
Monterey cypress see Cupressus
    macrocarpa
Monterey pine see Pinus radiata
Montrose, Duchess of 36, 38, 39
moor grass, purple see Molinia caerulea
Moore, Brett 108
Moore, Robert 160
morning glory see Ipomoea
mosaics 26
Mottistone Common 155
Mottistone Gardens 157–64, 188
Mount Stuart 35, 186
Mull, Isle of 125, 126–37, 187–8
Muncaster Castle 39
Munnings, Sir Alfred 157
Munro, John and Pauline 87, 95
Murray, Colonel 146, 149
Musa (banana) 39, 163, 167, 170
Myrtus (myrtle) 167

Narcissus (daffodil) 16–17
    N. 'Geranium' 16
    N. 'Golden Dawn' 16, 17
    N. 'Grand Primo' 16
    N. 'Matador' 16
    N. 'Moon Shadow' 16
    N. 'Scilly White' 16
    N. 'Soleil d'Or' 16
nasturtium see Tropaeolum
National Trust 160, 181, 184
National Trust for Scotland 39, 40, 52
Nelhams, Mike 21, 29, 30
nemesia 136
Nepeta (catmint) 158, 161
    N. 'Six Hills Giant' 118, 121, 121
Nerine
    N. sarniensis (Guernsey lily) 100, 101
    N. x versicolor 'Mansellii' 100
New Zealand Christmas tree see
    Metrosideros excelsa
New Zealand flax see Phormium tenax
Nicholson, Sir John and Lady Vivien 158,
    160, 161
Nicotiana (tobacco plant)
    N. mutabilis 170
    N. sylvestris 170
Nigella damascena (love-in-a-mist) 118, 185
    N.d. 'Miss Jekyll' 185, 185
Norfolk Island pine see Araucaria
    heterophylla
Nothofagus (southern beech) 39
Nymphaea (water lily) 104

obelisks 79, 184
Olea europaea (olive) 163
Olearia 17, 108, 140
    O. arborescens 130
    O. chathamica 130
    O. x haastii 170
    O. paniculata 104, 106, 118
    O. x scilloniensis 29
    O. traversii 90, 108, 130, 140
olive see Olea europaea
orchids 142, 143
    common spotted see Dactylorhiza fuchsii
    heath spotted see Dactylorhiza maculata
    lady's tresses see Spiranthes
        romanzoffiana
    lesser butterfly see Platanthera bifolia
Orkney 74–95, 187
Orkney Garden Trail 82, 187
Oronsay, Isle of 11, 138–43, 188

Oronsay Farm 138
Oronsay Priory 138–43, 188
Osborne House 155, 188
osmanthus 170
Osmunda regalis (royal fern) 70
Osteospermum
   O. 'Nairobi Purple' *28, 29*
   O. 'Pink Whirls' 95
   O. 'Tresco Peggy' *see O.* 'Nairobi Purple'
Owen, Neil 48
Oxalis pes-caprae (Bermuda buttercup) 15
Ozothamnus rosmarinifolius 'Silver Jubilee'
   132, *136*

Pachysandra terminalis 136
Paget, Paul 157–8
Palmer, Mike and Sue 84
palms 108, *162*, 163
   palm heath *see Richea pandanifolia*
pampas grass *see Cortaderia*
pansy, dwarf *see Viola kitaibeliana*
Papaver (poppy) 84, 95
   P. orientale (oriental poppy) 95
pavilions 150, *151*, 167, *167*, 170
pear 106
pelargonium 19, 136
Pelley, Le, family 114
   Susanne 113
penstemon 104, 160
Persicaria 161
   P. amplexicaulis 66
      P.a. 'Rosea' *82*
   P. bistorta (common bistort) *82*
petunia 158
phlox *132*
Phoenix canariensis (Canary Island date
   palm) 11, *23*, 26
Phormium 104, 108, 163
   P. tenax (New Zealand flax) 90, *111*
Phytophthora
   P. kernoviae 40
   P. ramorum 40
Picea sitchensis (sitka spruce) 146
pine *see Pinus*
pineapple lily *see Eucomis*
pink
   scented *see Dianthus*
   sea *see Armeria maritima*
Pinus (pine)
   P. pinea (Mediterranean stone pine) *111*
   P. radiata (Monterey pine) 20
Pittosporum
   P. crassifolium 16, 17, *17*
   P. tenuifolium 165
      P.t. 'Irene Paterson' 130
   P. tobira (Japanese mock orange) 170
plant-hunting 10, 20, 29, 36, 71
Plas Cadnant *59*, 60–73, 186–7
Plas Newydd 59, 187
Platanthera bifolia (lesser butterfly orchid)
   48, *143*, 143
Polemonium (Jacob's ladder) 84, *84*
   P. carneum 90
polygonatum 150
Polystichum (shield fern) 70
   P. setiferum (soft shield fern) *70*
Pope, Nori and Sandra 167
poppy *see Papaver*
Potentilla thurberi 'Monarch's Velvet' *82*
Price family 61–2, 70
pride of Madeira *see Echium candicans*
Primula 70
   P. pulverulenta 40, 44
Priory Garden 138–43, 188
privet *see Ligustrum ovalifolium*
Protea 19, 21, 108
   P. neriifolia 30
Prunus
   P. dulcis (almond) 158
   P. laurocerasus (cherry laurel) 61, 166
   P. serrulata (Japanese cherry) 149
   P. spinosa (blackthorn) 111

Pseudotsuga menziesii (Douglas fir) 48
Puya chilensis (Chilean puya) 26, *30*
pyracantha 104

Quercus ilex (holm oak) 26, 108, *111*, 118,
   121, 170
quince *see Cydonia oblonga*
Quoy of Houton, The 78, *82*, 187

red hot poker *see Kniphofia*
red valerian *see Centranthus ruber*
religious communities 11, 175
Repton, Humphry 59
Reseda odorata (mignonette) 185
Rheum palmatum 'Red Herald' 130
Rhododendron 38, 39, 40, 52, 53, 103, 104,
   142
   R. augustinii Electra Group 'Electra' *40*
   R. 'Britannia' x *R. elliotti see R.* 'Leo'
   R. Subsection *Cinnabarina* 53
   R. 'Colonel Rogers' 52
   R. concinnum x *R. concetenans* x *R.*
      cinnabarinum see R. Three Cs
   R. 'Earl of Athlone' x *R.* 'Glory of
      Leonardslee' 53
   R. 'Elsie Watson' *53*
   R. Subsection *Falconeri* 39
   R. fulvum 52
   R. Gigha Gem *53*
   R. 'Glory of Athlone' 53, *53*
   R. 'Glory of Littleworth' *40*
   R. Subsection *Grandia* 39
   R. hemsleyanum 40
   R. horlickianum 53
   R. 'Lady Berry' 53
   R. Lady Chamberlain Group 53
   R. 'Lady Horlick' 53
   R. Lady Roseberry Group 53
   R. 'Leo' 53
   R. luteum 49
   R. macabeanum 39, *40*
   R. Subsection *Maddennii* 39, 53
      R. maddenii hybrid *40*
   R. magnificum 39
   R. montroseanum 39
   R. 'Mrs James Horlick' 52, *53*
   R. niveum 40
   R. ponticum 40, 53, 61, *68*
   R. 'Songbird' 53
   R. Three Cs 53
   R. vernicosum hybrid *40*
Rhopalostylis sapida (Nikau palm) 23
Ring of Brodgar 77
Rock, Joseph 36
rock rose *see Cistus*
Rodgersia 95, *131*
   R. pinnata 'Perthshire Bronze' 130
Romneya coulteri (Californian tree poppy) 48
Rosa 82, 113, 114, *115*, *121*, 140, 158
   climbing 167
   English *167*
   wild 142
   R. banksiae 'Lutea' 118
   R. 'Betty Prior' 150
   R. Bonica 150, 160
   R. canina (dog rose) 165
   R. 'Climbing Lady Hillingdon' 118
   R. gallica
      R.g. var. *officinalis* (apothecary's rose)
      118, 140
      R.g. 'Versicolor' (rosa mundi) 118, 121
   R. Gertrude Jekyll 184
   R. Glad Tidings *115*
   R. glauca 132
   R. 'Killarney' *182*
   R. moyesii 132
   R. 'New Dawn' 132, 150
   R. 'Paul's Himalayan Musk' 132
   R. 'Penelope' 150
   R. 'Phyllis Bide' 66
   R. 'Rambling Rector' 118
   R. 'Roseraie de l'Haÿ' 160

Rosa (cont.)
   R. rugosa 140, 140
   R. Super Fairy *118*
   R. Tess of the d'Urbervilles *118*
   R. The Pilgrim *118*
   R. 'Tuscany Superb' *118*, 121
   R. 'Wedding Day' 111
   R. 'Zéphirine Drouhin' 182
rosa mundi *see R. gallica* 'Versicolor'
Rosmarinus (rosemary) 140, 167
Rothesay 35, 43
Rothschild, Lionel de 100
rowan *see Sorbus*
royal fern *see Osmunda regalis*
Royal Horticultural Society Partner Gardens
   43–9
Rudbeckia 182
   R. fulgida var. *speciosa* 182
runner beans 106

sage *see Salvia*
St Agnes, Island of 15, 16, 186
St Columba 138
St Cuthbert 175
St Martin's, Island of 15, *15*, 186
St Mary's, Island of 15, 16, *19*, 186
St Michael's Mount *9*
St Peter Port 100, 103
Salix (willow) 82
   S. fargesii 130
   S. magnifica 130
   S. nakamurana var. *yezoalpina* 136
salt damage 10
salt tree *see Halimodendron halodendron*
Salvia (sage) 19, *161*, 167
   S. 'Amistad' 136
santolina 182
Sark, Island of *9*, 98, 112–21, 187
Savill garden, The 53
saxifrage 35
Scabiosa caucasia 182
Scilly, Isles of 10–11, 12–31, 163, 186
Scotland: south-western islands 31–95, 186
Scots pine 35
Scott, Mencia and Peter 165–71
sculpture
   Gaia *29*
   Neptune *28*
sea holly *see Eryngium*
sea pink *see Armeria maritima*
seats *79*
seaweed 84
sedge *see Carex*
Sedum 66, 167
   S. telephium
      S.t. 'Munstead Red' 184
      S.t. 'Red Cauli' 136
Seely, General Jack 157
Seely, John 157
Seigneurie, La 112–21, 187
Seil, Isle of *11*, 144–51, 188
shell patterns 26
shield fern *see Polystichum*
sisyrinchum 84
sitka spruce *see Picea sitchensis*
Skye, Isle of 125
Smith, Augustus 20, 21
Smith, Fiona and Euan 87–90, 95
snapdragon *see Antirrhinum*
snow-in-summer *see Cerastium
   tomentosus*
snowdrop *see Galanthus*
soft shield fern *see Polystichum setiferum*
Sonchus arboreus (dandelion tree) 30
Sorbus (rowan)
   S. arranensis 35
   S. aucuparia 140
South Ronaldsay, Isle of *11*, 187
Spiranthes romanzoffiana (lady's tresses
   orchid) 143
spruce, sitka *see Picea sitchensis*
Stachys byzantina 182

Stenwood 187
strawberries 140, 184
Styrax japonica (Japanese snowbell) 70
sundial *121*
Sunninghill 53
sweet pea *see Lathyrus odoratus*
   perennial *see Lathryus latifolius*
sycamore *see Acer pseudoplatanus*

tamarix 130
Tasmannia lanceolata 130
Tavernor, Anthony 61, *62*, 66
Taxus (yew) 66, *66*, 69, 118
   T. baccata 'Fastigiata Robusta' 66
Taylor, George 52
Tazetta daffodil 16, *16*
teucrium 140
Thalictrum 150
   T. aquilegiifolium 82
   T. 'Elin' 130
   T. flavum 132
Thaxter, Celia 7, 11, 140
thistle, globe *see Echinops*
Thomas, Graham Stuart 66
Thymus
   T. polytrichus subsp. *britannicus* (wild thyme)
      143, *143*
Tilia (lime) 103
Till, Rupert *145*
tobacco plant *see Nicotiana sylvestris*
Todd, Mr 47
Todea barbara (king fern) 44, 47, *47*
Tooley, Michael and Rosanna 181
topiary *62, 69*
Torosay Garden 187
Trachycarpus fortunei (Chusan palm) 11
tree ferns *40, 44*
tree lupin *see Lupinus arboreus*
Tresco 15, 186
Tresco Abbey Garden 19–31, *38*, 39, 186
Tropaeolum (nasturtium) 84
Twr Maŵr *59*

Ulmus (elm) 15, 19, 54, 165

valerian *see Centranthus*
Vancouver Island 9
Veitch Nursery 71
Verbena bonariensis 167, 170
Verey, Rosemary 35
Viola kitaibeliana (dwarf pansy) 15
viper's bugloss *see Echium vulgare*

Walker, Harry 177–9
walled gardens *38, 62, 62*, 90, 113–14, 118, 121,
   121, 177, 179, 182
walnut *see Juglans*
water lily *see Nymphaea*
waterfalls 70, *73*, 148, 149
Western Australian Botanic Garden, Kings
   Park 26
Westray, Isle of *77*
Whistler, Rex 59
White House, Herm 108, *111*
White Island 7
Wight, Isle of 9, 152–71, 188
wild flowers 11, 143
willow *see Salix*
windbreaks 16, 82, 90, 108
winter's bark *see Drimys winterii*
wisteria 167
woodland 70, 121
Wynne, David *29*

yew *see Taxus*
Ynys Môn *see* Anglesey

Zantedeschia aethiopica (arum lily) *70*
zinnia 158

Island Gardens
© 2018 Quarto Publishing plc
Text © 2018 Jackie Bennett
Photographs © 2018 Richard Hanson
(with the exception of those listed right)

First published in 2018 by White Lion Publishing,
an imprint of The Quarto Group,
The Old Brewery, 6 Blundell Street,
London N7 9BH, United Kingdom
www.QuartoKnows.com

A catalogue record for this book is available from the British Library.

ISBN 978-0-7112-3975-3

Commissioning Editor: Helen Griffin
Designer: Anne Wilson
Project Editor: Joanna Chisholm

Printed and bound in China

9 8 7 6 5 4 3 2

Brimming with creative inspiration, how-to projects and useful
information to enrich your everyday life, Quarto Knows is a
favourite destination for those pursuing their interests and
passions. Visit our website and dig deeper with our books into
your area of interest: Quarto Creates, Quarto Cooks, Quarto
Homes, Quarto Lives, Quarto Drives, Quarto Explores, Quarto
Gifts, or Quarto Kids.

ACKNOWLEDGMENTS

The author would like to sincerely thank The Society of Authors/
Authors' Foundation, which supported this project with a grant.
With grateful thanks to all the owners and gardeners featured in the
book. In addition she would like to thank the following individuals
who helped in many different ways: Alec Cormack and Joanna
Macpherson of Attadale Gardens (www.attadale.com) and Discover
Scottish Gardens (www.discoverscottishgardens.com) whose
advisers guided her to various Scottish gardens; Arran: Sarah Earney
(Brodick Estate); Gigha: Susan Allan, Helen Lear, Alasdair MacNeill,
Malcolm MacNeill, Elaine Morrison, Jacqui Smith and Amy Wilson.
Also to Helen Haugh, who researched Achamore Gardens as part
of a University of London MA; Guernsey: Caroline Allisette (Floral
Guernsey), Jill Bishop (Plant Heritage Guernsey) and Matt Trimmer
(Fermain Valley Hotel); Holy Island: Carol Macleod, Nick Lewis
(Lindisfarne Castle); Isle of Wight: Mike and Helen Snow (Holmelea,
Brighstone); Oronsay: The Colburn Family, Margaret and Duncan
McDougall, Steve Glue (gardener) and Andy Knight of the RSPB. Also
to Penelope Hobhouse who shared her experience of designing the
garden; Orkney: John and Sarah Welburn (Crystal Brook, Orphir);
Sark: Jo Birch (La Seigneurie), Pauline Mallinson (Beau Sejour);
Tresco: Mike Nelhams and the staff of the Tresco Estate.

The quotation on page 7, from Celia Thaxter, *An Island Garden*,
1894, is from http://digital.library.upenn.edu/women/thaxter/
garden/garden.html; https://www.shoalsmarinelaboratory.org/.

The photographer would like to thank Steve Betts, Russell
Donnelly and Nigel Wilkinson for their help.

PICTURE ACKNOWLEDGMENTS

All photographs by Richard Hanson except for the following.
Image Science & Analysis Laboratory, NASA Johnson Space Center 4-5.
Shutterstock: Peter Turner Photography 11 centre; Andrew Roland
14-15; Daniel Heighton 21 right; Peter Turner Photography 23; Andrew
Roland 24-5; BigRoloImages 29 left; James McDowall 32-3; LouieLea
38 top; EQRoy 38 bottom; Snowshill 56-7; Peter Turner Photography
68 bottom; Marbury 91 top row, second from left; David Woods 74-5;
ChrisNoe 76-7; haraldmuc 96-7; Kiev.Victor 100; HonzaM 125 bottom;
Laurence Baker 152-3; Michael Conrad 174-5.
Biodiversity Heritage Library for the king fern illustration from
The Gardeners' Chronicle 47.
Charles Hawes 66, 67.
Jill Bishop, Plant Heritage Guernsey 101 top.
Alamy 176-7.
Carol Macleod 178 top left.